Aiblins

New Scottish Political Poetry

EDITED BY
KATIE AILES AND SARAH PATERSON

Luath Press Limited
EDINBURGH
www.luath.co.uk

First published 2016

ISBN: 978-1-910745-84-7

The paper used in this book is recyclable. It is made from low chlorine pulps produced in a low energy, low emissions manner from renewable forests.

Printed and bound by
Bell & Bain Ltd., Glasgow

Typeset in 10.5 point Sabon by
3btype.com

Contents

3

Acknowledgements

We are grateful to Luath Press for publishing this anthology and for their support throughout this process.

Thank you to the National Library of Scotland for hosting the Poetic Politics conference in 2015, and especially to Amy Todman for her hard work in helping to make it a reality. We are also grateful to Amy for allowing us access to the Referendum Collection and helping us to curate our pop-up exhibition during the conference. Thank you to all of those who participated in that event and supported us as we went forward with this book which emerged from that wonderful day in September.

Huge thanks are due to the sub-editorial team, who dedicated their time and expertise to discussing the many submissions to this anthology and who helped us to shape the final result. David Kinloch, Lotte Mitchell Reford, Ruairidh Maciver, Amy Todman, Stewart Smith, Nia Clark, AK Harris: thank you for your care, consideration, and inspiration! This collection is book-ended by the wise words of David Kinloch and Robert Crawford and we'd like to express our gratitude for these contributions, which have made this collection complete.

We also owe a deep debt of gratitude to those who made the inclusion of Gaelic poems and translations of poems into Gaelic possible. Ruairidh McIver, thank you so much for patiently going through the Gaelic submissions with us and giving your honest opinions. Calum L MacLeòid, thank you very much for thoughtfully translating four of the English poems into Gaelic for this book, and for your willingness to join us on this experiment.

Thanks as well to the many individuals and groups who helped us to spread our call for submissions, including Scottish PEN, the Scottish Poetry Library and the Association for Scottish Literary Studies.

Thank you to the University of Glasgow New Initiatives Fund and the Tannahill Fund for generously supporting this project and enabling the payment of the artists involved, and to the University of Glasgow for hosting the sub-editorial workshop.

And of course, thank you so much to all of the poets who submitted work to this project. It was a delight to read your work and to shape it into this book. We very much hope that you enjoy it.

Foreword

AS I WRITE, it has been announced that the Syrian city of Aleppo now has no access to water supplies. It prepares to endure further bombardment. Our screens fill with the evidence of gross acts of human depravity: children with limbs blown off look at us numbly or with corrosive suspicion. Four hundred thousand Syrians lie dead. Entire populations stream across borders to escape the fanaticism of monotheistic fascists, tribal dictators or economic deprivation.

Global climate change has already had possibly irreversible effects on the environment. Glaciers have shrunk, ice on rivers and lakes dissolves earlier, animal species are on the verge of extinction.

> Things fall apart; the centre cannot hold;
> Mere anarchy is loosed upon the world,
> The blood-dimmed tide is loosed, and everywhere
> The ceremony of innocence is drowned;

These great lines by WB Yeats take the measure of the enormities that confronted an earlier generation. They frame and focus through the vivid ceremonies of language itself and stand, as perhaps only poems can do, as the most intense form of mnemonic, sounding out the ramifications of what has happened and anticipating what may be to come.

Measured against this barometer the onus on poets to respond adequately to the times they live in and bear witness to is considerable. Although it may seem to some that the events – the referendum on independence, the galvanising of Scottish political consciousness – that prompted this particular anthology of political verse comprise little more than a local squabble among the denizens of one of the richest nations on earth, a hullabaloo on the periphery of everything significant, it is not for our generation to judge. And there have been times, certainly, over the last few years, sunk in the inanities of media coverage, when one has been tempted to cry, 'Look up, look around, stop navel gazing!'.

It is to the credit of some of the poets in this anthology that they too seem to have experienced an element of exasperation. They have looked up, looked beyond Scotland and then looked back at Scotland again, placing it in a more global perspective and carefully considering its own past, its own complicity in empire and exploitation. And there is a timely acknowledgement too by some of the fragility of the land on which we stand and call home. I was struck by the large number of narrative poems, by the apparent need to break this moment in Scotland's history down into the elements of story so as to better understand it. Intense lyric concentration is rarer; the sudden startling image that will offer a clarifying insight perhaps needs more time and more distance from the events themselves. What is beyond question is that each of the poems selected for this anthology cares enough about the events it tackles to try to shape them into memorable language. Their success is a measure of their care. And it is to the editors' credit that they have striven so hard in a world saturated by social media and the soundbite to salvage and curate these responses to a memorable and possibly crucial phase of Scotland's history.

David Kinloch

Introduction

THE TEXT IN YOUR hands is a selection of new Scottish
political poetry. The poems in this collection reflect the
tumultuous, rapidly evolving nature of contemporary
Scottish politics. They also stand as a testament to the deep
engagements Scottish poets are making with the political
landscape today, not only by reflecting on current events
through their poetry but also by issuing provocations
which reframe and challenge conventional assumptions.

The idea to publish this volume was sparked by a
conference we co-organised in September 2015, entitled
'Poetic Politics: Culture and the 2014 Independence
Referendum, One Year On'. The conference was held at
the National Library of Scotland and was possible due to
the efforts of its Referendum Curator, Amy Todman.
Opened by the Scottish Cabinet Secretary for Culture,
Fiona Hyslop, it featured artists, academics, cultural event
organisers, politicians and engaged citizens discussing the
legacy of the referendum and its ongoing reverberations in
Scottish culture. Robert Crawford's keynote speech for the
conference was the perfect opening to the day, and
provides the perfect conclusion to this collection.

At the conference, we recognised that there was an
impressive level of artistic engagement with the referendum
– whether Yes, No, Maybe or Neither – but that this
material wasn't necessarily captured or published in an
accessible, sustainable manner. So much of the poetry,
music and performance sparked by the independence
debate had only a fleeting, ephemeral existence during the
referendum campaign, performed live or lost in private
notebooks or social media sites, considered no longer

'relevant' following the vote. As researchers studying this body of work, and as poets ourselves, we considered it important to gather and publish this material, both for posterity and because we wanted to ensure some of this brilliant poetry didn't go unnoticed. To specifically gather poetry which may not have received the attention we believe it deserved, we requested submissions that had not previously been released in book form, and preferably that had not been published at all until now. As a result, this collection comprises unearthed gems we are overjoyed to be bringing to light.

Even in the short time between the 2014 referendum and the conference that we held one year later, the creative energy generated during the lead up to the vote was continuing to flourish in different ways. As a result, we did not intend for the collection to simply be a reflection upon the referendum campaigns. Rather, we wished for it to be a snapshot of contemporary Scotland's creative response to many facets of its political landscape, complete with poets' reflections on the past, a frustration or engagement with the present and hope (or trepidation) for the future. We left the definition of 'political' intentionally broad: poems were invited on any subject the poet deemed political, from any perspective, due to our recognition that often the most powerful 'political' poetry is that which approaches the topic from a less overtly political angle.

We left the definition of the Scottish poet similarly open – poets need not be 'Scottish' in any blood- or birth-related sense in order to submit, as long as they had been resident in Scotland at some point. As 'foreigners' ourselves – an American and a New Zealander – who arrived on the eve of the independence referendum and have since made this extraordinary place our home, we felt it crucial that the definition of the Scottish poet be as inclusive and welcoming as we have found the country itself to be.

Scotland's internationalist attitude is certainly on show here: Scottish culture and identity as demonstrated in these poems was often not located within Scotland at all. We received a number of poems written outwith Scotland, and even more which looked beyond Scotland or the United Kingdom for political inspiration. These poems reflect not an insular nation, but rather one deeply concerned with the world beyond its borders.

As the project involved publishing a diversity of Scottish voices, we found it necessary to have the content of the book selected by people with a diversity of perspectives on contemporary Scottish life. We gathered a sub-editorial team comprising figures from across the UK, with different backgrounds and ideas on contemporary Scottish culture, which led to some rather vigorous debate at times about how the book should work and what it should include. We are very grateful to this team for their support and for frequently shifting our opinions on what material would fit best and how to frame it. All poems were reviewed blind with the poets' names removed. In putting together a political anthology, the editors and sub-editors were inevitably faced with the challenges of being as impartial as possible; however, impartiality cannot always be the same as balance. In 2015, we set out aiming to organise a conference that represented Yes and No views on the referendum in equal measure. Ultimately, however, we realised we would not be able to do so in light of the body of work at hand. When it came to selecting work for this collection, we were faced with the same conundrum both relating to the 2014 referendum and to many other topics. Our goal in curating this collection therefore, was to prioritise work which was original and nuanced, and which approached these contentious issues from less obvious angles than Yes or No, For or Against, Pro or Anti.

The submissions weren't just diverse in terms of perspective, but in voices too. We were delighted to receive poems in a wide range of languages, including Scots, Gaelic and Shetlandic in addition to English. We hope that this book reflects the linguistic diversity of its submissions, and we are deeply grateful to those who helped us to make this possible through their provision of translations. Early in the editorial process we made the decision to flip the way in which poems have traditionally been translated in anthologies of Scottish verse. Rather than providing translations of Gaelic poems into English, as has become the standard, we decided instead to translate four English poems into Gaelic and leave the Gaelic poems untranslated. We hope that, for Gaelic and English speakers alike, this project provides an opportunity to reflect upon the political and social role of translation in today's cultural economy.

We have attempted to curate this volume in a way that reflects the themes which were clearly important to the poets who submitted. One topic immediately stood out as being in the forefront of poets' minds: the refugee crisis. Scores of poets approached this subject from many different angles, but what surprised us was the uniformity of the message we seemed to be receiving, to 'open the doors' in the words of Edwin Morgan's timeless poem for the Scottish Parliament. Several poets approached the issue from a uniquely Scottish perspective, drawing comparisons between suffering in Syria, Greece or Calais with that of Scotland's own diaspora. Some did not shy away from the other side of that coin, and images of empire also filter through, revealing a Scotland deeply concerned with its own complicity. History and the ways in which the past resonates with the present was a far more common theme than either of us anticipated and that is reflected in this collection. Looking to the future, we received a wealth of beautiful ecopoetic pieces which highlight our fragility as part of the changing landscape of Scotland itself.

Conversely, there were also subjects we expected to receive plenty of work on, but which became conspicuous by their near absence: class, party politics, land reform, sexuality, employment or the National Health Service for example. It became apparent that a topic's prevalence in the headlines did not necessarily translate to its prevalence in poetry. It is an immense challenge to write political poetry where the polemic does not overwhelm the lyric, and it is possible that some of these issues do not easily lend themselves to well-crafted verse. In making our selections, we have tried to keep in mind the advice given to us by Robert Crawford at the outset of the project, to 'not let the politics overwhelm the poetry'. As poets ourselves – and ones who frequently comment on the political in our own work – we have found this process invaluable for developing our own sense of the shadowy border between poetry and polemic.

The Scotland you'll find in this collection is far from single-minded or self-assured. Aside from the plurality of voices – and there certainly is that – there is a sense of indecision, of swithering, grasping to find a solid consensus or identity. Perhaps that is why, when we came across Stewart Sanderson's brilliantly concise poem 'Aiblins', which defines Scotland in these terms, we couldn't imagine a better title.

Even between the call for submissions and this book finding its way into your hands, much will have changed in Scotland's political landscape. In only the weeks between the close of submissions and the final assembly of the manuscript, the United Kingdom voted to leave the European Union and found itself with a new Prime Minister. But one thing we love about the poetry collected here is that it does not shy away from change and the unknown in political life: it celebrates it and confronts it.

We passionately believe that art has an important role in the political world. It can commentate on contemporary issues whilst simultaneously reminding us of our past and its relevance, as the poets do in 'Korean Letters', 'Viewpoints', 'Ciocharan' or 'Old School Maps'. It can bring our attention to issues we've never thought about before, as Henry Bell does in 'Alice Coy Told Me How'. It can render the invisible visible, as in Chris Boyland's 'The Chair.' It can introduce new words into our lexicon, broadening our understanding of language as Arun Sood's 'Divali in Kessock' does. It can help put our own lived experience into new perspectives, allowing us to see it differently, something achieved by the poets of the referendum in this volume. It also serves as a record of thoughts and feelings which *Hansard* or history books struggle to recall, and we hope that this volume will serve as a form of record for Scotland at this incredible period of time in its history. More so than anywhere else we've seen, poetry and politics seem to be natural bedfellows here in Scotland. Poetry has helped us to understand and interpret the nuance amid the seismic shifts beneath us, and we hope this volume can be a part of that process for others.

Finally, we're both firm believers that poetry should not be confined to the page (not to denigrate the volume you're holding right now!). As a companion to this book, we've asked the poets included to submit recordings of themselves reading their work, and we're publishing these pieces freely and accessibly through our YouTube channel.

You may find them by searching 'Poetic Politics' or through our website. We hope you enjoy them, as we have.

Katie Ailes and Sarah Paterson
Glasgow, September 2016

Aiblins

Stewart Sanderson

Like Scotland, slightly
synthetic and in a state
of indecision.

'S Mathaid

Translation of 'Aiblins' by Calum L MacLeòid

Coltach ri Alba, car
Coineallach agus na stàit
Neo-chinnteachd.

Territory

AC Clarke

Somewhere on the high moors over Carter Bar
you can stand with one foot in each country
the wind bending grassblades
to the English side, the Scottish side
while a bird hops to and fro
across an invisible line
singing its boundaries.

A Highland Favour

Brian Johnstone

Chrome was the thing. A bumper and grill
fit to polish, trim you could see your face in,
once the air kill of '50s holiday roads,

squashed corpses of midges and wasps,
was swabbed off. You knew you'd been up
to the Highlands by that, but better

was heather plucked from a verge-side bog,
the favour each homeward-bound car
would display; a wilting cockade tucked

under the bonnet of Singer and Sunbeam,
Hillman and Ford. A sign that they'd steered
down passing place roads, sheep dodging

their way through the braes for a fortnight
at some but an' ben. Back home, it was down
to the chrome of the grill, its emblem

reflecting belief in the north. Old Scotland
lashed to the bumper, a favour the future's
slipstream forgot, and swabbed off.

Overheard on a bus in Aberdeen

Mandy Macdonald

> *– Oh no! I've lost my travel pass!*
> *– You've lost your tribal past?*

Well, that too,
now you come to mention it:
I am so far from my ochre deserts,
my dawdling, tawny rivers,
my tangled harbours,
my thirsty grey-leaved eucalypts.

My history is smeared on the landscape there,
map and dream knitted in ages past but never gone
from rocks and stars, beasts and birds,
the yarn of songlines winding, binding past to present.

But I have no free pass to the past
where I must pay to go walkabout now,
not barefoot but hiking-booted in my own country;
I do not stride the songlines, tall and swift,
no, I creep in metal baggage, winged and wheeled
and new and safe
and paid for.

* * *

There is another history I know: I am writing it now,
on the cellphone flicking coloured light in my face.
I stand umbrella'd
in a rainy Scottish street at midnight, impelled
by some memory far older than I can calculate,
urgently to set this telling down.

Inside this small, smooth tessera, shiny-beetle-black,
that fits the hand as well as a stone skinning knife,
there's a grain of tantalum, older than all the songlines,
silent, latent under ancient rock paintings,

then, torn up from my land,
yanked, sifted, strained
from millions of tons of it,
from Greenbushes, Wodgina
upheaved, convulsed, raped.

And yet, without that scintilla
I could not write like this, standing
in the dark street, in the rain, half a planet away,
could not tell the story.

Family History: The Accent

Hilary Birch

1

I lost my accent one hot summer at the age of ten, just
  north of Christchurch.
We were heading back from Kaikoura after Christmas, via
  Hurunui, Waipara, and Kaiapoi,
when
juddering across the Waimak bridge, the Morris swerved to
  avoid a sheep and luggage
tumbled from the roof.
Dad stopped the car. We watched the torrent whirl our
  cases out to sea and with them went the ten Oor Wullie
  annuals, all our Jimmy Shands, the family kilts, the
  teapot Uncle Ronnie liberated from the Caly on VJ Day.

2

The Mother (*weeping*):	That teapot was all that remained to me of my ain folk.
The infant chorus (*singing*):	No moa, no moa, it's gone and there aint no moa.
The Mother:	You kids are nae comfort. It's all your fault, Hilry. It was your job to see to the roof rack. Ach, you're aye careless and a disappointment.
The Oldest Girl:	Strewth Ma, I don't reckon it was all down to me...
The Mother:	Dinna you speak to me in that coorse accent, you cow cockie, you antipodean tink.

3

Struck dumb, I buttoned my lip and bit my tongue.
A little voice said: Yer on yer own, girlie. You'll jist hae tae
    learn tae speak nice.

4

The Queen was my model. Her Christmas message had
    impressed us all.
We'd listened sweating in our kilts after the turkey dinner,
    Dad standing to attention with
his thumbs down the seams of his big shorts – 'the Queen,
    God Bless Her', Mam sniffling and plying her tartan
    hanky – 'Prince Charles was born just after you, Hilry'.

5

I know what you're thinking. You don't have to say it.
I killed my accent.
Yes, it's true, I admit it   Yeah   but it was self-defence,
    I reckon   Aye. Right.

Cìocharan

Marcas Mac an Tuairneir

Air bòrd na luinge,
Rinn e bhòidse,
Thairis air fairsingeachd a' chuain.

Aig uchd a mhàthar,
Ann am plaide clòtha,
Cìocharan a' dèanamh deoc.

Srùbag, srùbag.
Gabh gach boinneag uileag,
Gabh blasad
Air bainne lanntair do thùis.

Foghidinn sna ciudhan,
An eilean nan deòirean,
Far an do nochd gach gineal na cruinne.

Naoi ceistean air fhichead,
Cìreadh son snigean,
Àireamhachd air gach sgillinn ruaidh.

Clambraid is cabhag
Gach gin bhochd a' lorg,
A cuid,
San dùthaich ùr-nodha.

Ann an gabhaltas salach
Cùl-shràid Nuadh-Eabhraig,
Co-sheirm eadar tàirneanachd is caoineadh.

Fan air do chasan,
Gabh ri cleachdaidhean, gnàthasan,
Gach briathar do mhuinntire ùire.

Bà thu, Bà thu.
Gabh gach boinneag uileag,
Gabh blasad
Air bainne lanntair do thùis.

Lìon do bhrù,
Le bangaid an domhain,
Nas blàsta na garbhag is buntàta.

Tog ar lanntair as ùr,
A rèir meudachd matamataig,
A rèir luaithre na sgeulachd nad chuimhne.

Cosnaich is cosg
An notaichean uaine,
Gach dolar.
Ceannaich do dhualchas air ais.

Grinnich is finich e,
Meudaich na mion-phuingean.
Dreach dathan an deilbh-tìre àrsaidh.

Cleachd thu an clò,
Son deise chiataich do chliù,
Le clachan-lèig is boillsg de gach seòrs'.

Innis dhuinn, nach innis thu dhuinn.
Gach loidhn' ar làmh-sgrìobhainn,
Gach nòs,
'S tu cìocharain, a chruthaich ar fine.

Picture of Girl and Small Boy (Gaza, 2014)

Marjorie Lotfi Gill

I would like to tell her not to wear such flimsy shoes,
that rubble contains the whole spectrum of knowable
and unknowable dangers: sheets of metal, ripped
to knife's edge, live wires, bloated arms still reaching

for light. Her hair, scraped back into a ponytail,
is open to sky; remnants of buildings filter down
one concrete chunk at a time, and the midday bells
of rockets ring out above her. She carries a boy

on her still-narrow hips, his legs entwined around
her yellow dungarees. Like a rodeo rider, his left arm
grips her shoulder to steady himself, or her,
while his torso reels back and away; his body is asking

to slow down, to turn back. Instead, her eyes comb
the ground for a next step, fingers of her free hand
curled into a claw, as if to frighten off whatever
is coming, what she somehow knows is ahead.

Vatersay 1853/ Kos 2015

Hugh McMillan

The boats go out,
come back with their catch,
bundles, boxes, bodies,
returned to the barren lands
and buried in a pit.
When Autumn gales lash
the beach thin as a smile
we find children lying
in the shallows,
kissing the sea.

Bhatarsaigh 1853 / Kos 2015

Hugh McMillan
Translation of 'Vatersay 1853/Kos 2015'
by Calum L MacLeòid

Siùbhlaidh na bàtaichean,
is tillidh le làd iad,
paisgean, cisteachan, cuirp,
air an tilleadh gu tìrean seasg
is adhlaichte ann an sloc.
Gaoth fhogarach a' sgiùrsadh
na tràghad cho tana ri gàire
lorgaidh sinn clann nan laighe
anns an tanalachd
a' toirt pòg chun na mara.

Bethlehem-Glasgow

Irene Hossack

Not born at the same time,
or even conceived together,
but choosing to be paired.
Dizygotic,
are we psychic
as twins might be?
Do we delight
in each other's triumphs,
feel what happens in the other's streets,
shriek at each other's losses?
We were founded
on Christian miracles,
cities of David and Mungo,
flourishing, and yet divided
through broken branches
of the same tree.
Our dear green place
reaches out to your little town,
breaking through the walls
you did not build.

Viewpoint*

AC Clarke

Look up in Glasgow – what pinnacles of venture
crown spire and turret: merchantmen ride the skyline,
sails set to the gallant breeze, the globe,
pressed into service as a trader's finial,

tops soaring ambition, every skythrust
roars money, money, money. Walk in George Square
or past the dunce-cap Duke in Queen Street
to see the heart of old ship-laden wealth –

a marble heart and one that fed itself
on comfortable lies, didn't look deep
into the holds to see the cargo stashed
or smell the stench of living coffins crammed

with marketable bodies. The splash of those
thrown overboard couldn't be heard as far
as Glassford's drawing room where a black flunkey
waited behind the chair his master sat in,

brought his mistress' footstool, faded
out of the picture (or was painted out)
with no-one giving him a second thought
till now, when Glasgow after long amnesia

looks up and honours those who built it high,
carried it on bent backs like telamons,
or foundered in that Golden Triangle
where lives were cheapened. What remains of them?

A few brave memoirs and the inventories
in which inflicted names march down the page:
Gibbon, young and able, Billy ditto,
Archie ditto, Laurie – Mullato – infirm ...

---

* The painting referred to (by Archibald McLaughlan) is of the
  wealthy Glaswegian tobacco merchant John Glassford and his
  family. It included a black manservant standing behind Glassford
  but his image was either painted over, or has naturally faded.

Sealladh

AC Clarke
Translation of 'Viewpoint' by Calum L MacLeòid

Coimhead a-nìos an Glaschu – abair àirdean iomairte
a chrùnas gach spiric is turraid: marsantan a' siubhal na fàire
seòil mu sgaoil air oiteig euchdach, an domhan,
sparrte air mhuinntireas mar chrùn do cheannaichean,
na mullaichean air glòir-mhiann, gach sleagh a' gairm
airgead, airgead airgead. Coisich an Ceàrnag Sheòrais
no seachad Diùc na Bonaide air Sràid na Bànrighinn
gus cridhe seann bheartais nam bàtaichean fhaicinn,
cridhe marmor, cridhe a reamhraich fhèin
air breugan cofhurtail, nach tug sùil
a-nuas chun tuill far an tiodhlaichte am bathar
is nach d' fhuair fàileadh nan cisteachan-laighe bèo, pùcte
le cuirp fhèilleil. Cha chluinneadh plub a rinn iadsan
a chaidh thilgeil leis a' chliathaich idir ann an
seòmar-chuideachd Glassford, far na dh'fheith
sgalag dhubh air cùlaibh cathair a mhaighstir,
a bheir stòl-coise a bhana-mhaighstir, a dh'aognaich
às an dealbh (no a chaidh a pheantadh thairis)
gun nochdadh air aire duine sam bith
chun ìre seo, agus coimheadaidh Glaschu suas,
an ceann dìochuimhne fhada, agus molaidh i iadsan a thog
gu h-àrd i, a ghiùlain i air dromannan crùbte mar telemon
no a chaidh fodha anns an Triantan òir
far an saoraicheadh beathannan. Dè mhaireas dhaibhsan?
Cuimhneachain bheaga is maoin-chunntasan
far an caismich ainmean leònte sìos na duilleige:
Gibbon, òg is comasach, Uilleam ceudna,
Eàirdsidh ceudna, Laurie – lachdannach – anfhann...

Old School Maps

Brian Johnstone

They kept them in the attic store – behind the epidiascope,
and posters from the polio campaign – abandoned
as outdated, but too well made

to ever be thrown out. Scrolled tightly round their poles,
and tied with faded strips of tape, these maps
were of the old school. Just finding them

evoked that rattle as pole and canvas unscrolled one on one,
the pink of empire washed across the space
like pride at what was done

for those pronounced unwilling or unable to take such steps
themselves. A notion far too tightly rolled
to ever be thrown out, as if

subjugation was equivalent to defeating a disease, each map
a beam shone through an obsolete appliance
not yet entirely given up to rust.

Cuimhneachadh Ceud Bliadhna o Mhurt James Connolly

Greg MacThòmais

Ceangailte ris a' chathair seo, ciorramach. Chan èirich mi
   tuilleadh.
Sruth dheur a thuiteas, chan ann bhom shùil
A lìonas eilean
A mhaslaicheas lebhiathan.
Brag fòirneirt
Agus, an sin, teàrnaidh sìth car briste.
Cha ghabh anam a ghlacadh no lèirsinn a losgadh sa
   mhochthrath.
Bha mise nam shaighdear air gnothach na h-ìompaireachd
   uair, coltach riut fhèin.

Jackie's ma Auntie

Valerie Wilson

Oan a gie dreich nicht
still she stauns airm raised
strong in defiance.
Jist a statue now,
wi' seagull shit oan
'n' drum vandalised
b' random morons.
Aw bit back then –
hairt pumpin' the blood
roun' her 'hale boady,
as she leads the roar
o' 'Nae Militia'
cairit loud oan wind
ower rooftops 'n' wa's whur
bairns sit as lookoots
beatin' her drum an'
marchin' up's main street
'til a' wir chased doon
an' Jackie lay deid
wi' ha'dozen mair
a bloody day t'was
Tranent Massacre.

Korean Letters*

David Cameron

1

Nettie, your fears of the Formosa Straits
Were unfounded,
As we sailed on the opposite side.
I have sent you a postcard of Singapore.

2

I'm in the transit camp at Kure.
I don't know how long I'll be here.
So until you receive a definite address,
There is no point in writing.

3

One hears of the atrocities,
Some isolated cases
Of British soldiers foully murdered.
I suppose some of these tales are true.

4

The school children all wear long trousers,
Buttoned-to-the-neck jackets, and peaked caps.
The women, except for the prostitutes,
Wear long skirts with a high waistline.

5

Language is a barrier but I have tried
To carry on a conversation
With pidgin English and signs –
Mostly with signs.

6

The Glasgow Fair will be in full swing by now.
Just think, if I was at home,
I would probably be away myself.

Now I'm in Korea, 11,000 miles from home.

7

I was deeply grieved to hear
Of the sudden death of Mrs Finlayson.
There must be some reason for birth and death
Which conforms to a pattern in the universe.

8

Glad you are both keeping well.
No need to worry about me, Ma.
I'll come home safe and sound.
I've still got the key to let myself in.

* Assembled verbatim from fragments of letters written by the poet's
  father, George Cameron, while on National Service in Korea.

Four Allegories of Independence

Brian Johnstone

1949
Railings Wasted

Scarce a wall outside a pre-war house
does not betray the past in some way

with these lines of sores, lead long ago
poured in to set what's left just rows

of stumps, still clear near to a century
since amputation proved to be the fate

of railings everywhere. No matter
that the iron languished year on year

in depots, dumps and stores. Its time
would come as surely as necessity

will always find its place. In this case
ballast in the holds of empire, rusting

right away, and come the white heat
of the future, science-led, the PM said

would forge a new land – bottoming
for ring roads, leading nowhere fast.

1979
A Stand of Thistles

As if guarding the crossroads,
a stand of thistles fronts an empty sky,
the stretch of green

between them and the road,
a swathe where mowers have cleared
a view of either way.

Dusty from the heat,
the grime of passing traffic marking
those cut closest to the edge, they seem

no worse for weather dry as this
as from the action of the blade,
each barb: a test, a challenge to the end.

1997
National Trust

The dust that's hoovered up from fabric,
brushed from ornaments and artefacts

is all that's left, a consolation prize
for pasts on which the sun (they said)

would never set. What's fading here
is empire, nothing less, fading

in these sagging sofas, threadbare chairs
roped off to keep the public's weariness

from any chance of rest. Fading even
as the dust sheets carefully are spread

at summer's end, the curtains all
are drawn against the light, and gauze

across the vacuum's mouth arrests,
for one more season, certain slow decay.

A Hedge in the Making

In the verges, field margins, round the edge of the wood,
they're everywhere, growing apace, a clamour of saplings
in last season's leaves – withered and dead to the wind –

but stems supple, straight with new life. These we ease
from the soil – beech hedge in the making – barrow down
to the end of the plot, puddle in with design that our care

for the taking requires. No boundary but a gesture of need,
a quest for the shelter we found wanting for years and here,
with the promise of growth in the stems, can see marking

a lot unconfined. Hedged in, there are ever gaps in the line
where views of the distance are still to be seen, but stitched
now to the nap of this place, hemmed by the turn of a spade.

September 2014

Hugh McMillan

On top of Dunreggan,
the sky is white and burns like a crown.
Far off, a helicopter
hangs over a wood,
its gruffness the only sound
apart from wind,
which is not a sound but a freshness,
a kind of freedom on the skin.
There's poetry here
the land is clodded with it,
the great hills images to be broken up,
the grass streaming like words.
I am the only person here,
this heady day,
and I am balancing the sun
on one finger,
holding everything at bay
for a dream.

Friday the Nineteenth

Katy Ewing

A week ago your old work car had had it, spent
from twelve hard years of trusted running,
heavy loads and dirty jobs.
You'd called me, breathless, saying:
'Bad news, the Skoda died'
and only later let on that its snapping axle
nearly sent you under the wheels of a bus.

Today we'd woken late, knowing already
the future had been sold. Shattered
after last night's internet spectacle:
two guys streaming live, showing in real time
what the TV wasn't. Switching back and forth
between the cheery singing crowd in Freedom Square
and a Glasgow counting station, hushed,
pent up revelry and expectation rife
before the many crushing blows, serial hits.
At each result the sickening hoorays, applause,
of state-propping, self-serving career politicians
and their retinues, as if their horse had come in
and the champagne was already on ice.

A grim realisation settled
and eventually we went to bed.
Later, we heard Labour had danced their glee
with Tories on the Royal Yacht.

Now, sunk deep in grief, more painful, gut-deep,
than either of us had expected,
we'd gone to town as a distraction,
to find a second-hand van; life goes on.

Still, we kept seeing saltires everywhere
and a three letter word steeped in meaning,
much more than a campaign.
At first, like most, we'd been reluctant
to label ourselves or seem to wear colours,
not keen to be seen as hardliners, flag-wavers
– even nation-state believers.

But for weeks, these tiny badges had been key;
passing strangers would see each other's eyes,
heads held high, sometimes surprised
by who was on your side.
Admitting to the world that this was just,
a simple truth, a legitimate path,
the first steps to something better.
And we believed it could be
no matter what they called us.

As we walked to the car at one sales yard,
a white transit drove past, official 'Yes' large
across its back, driver's window open.
I gave him a thumbs-up for a past camaraderie
and he saw and replied with a shrug, a wave,
a sorry smile, as if bearing the weight
of responsibility alone.

And then he was gone, out of sight,
and there was nothing we could say.

Ouroboros

Jane Frank

We're not afraid
of the serpent.
Our intricate memories,
like lace,
will stretch and hold,
help us navigate
as we ride its curved back
to the horizon.
Grey will turn to white heat,
the green of home just a whisper
like the wash inside a shell.
We'll shed old skin
among the gum and wattle,
metamorphose into summer,
understand inside out
what it means to be home.

Hauntology

Roddy Shippin

it is not glaciation
which ridged these hills

furrows by Leverburgh
refusing to sink back

conceal fists of harvest
                        overhead

peat vibrating beneath grass
half cut

by the rocks
an acne of limpets

& seaweed once combed by crofters
when the ground yielded

too little

leave behind

Alec Finlay

leave behind the moss of cladhan

deep hollow

leave behind the profile of canup

the cantle

leave behind the spate of dubh-ghlais

dark burn

leave behind an impression on drumargettie

the silvery ridge

leave behind the blue of ruighe an lìn

flax shieling

leave behind the glow by allt an beal

the broom burnie

leave behind mottled cruaidh-leac

hill of hard flag-stones

leave behind astringent loinn-na-biorag

the glade of tormentil

leave behind a watersplash in allt ghealain

sparrow burn

leave behind the refreshment of sugh fhiorag

the pure-nectar well

leave behind the stink of breunalach

place that reeks

leave behind the scent of am beitheachann

the birch-bit wood

leave behind all thought of mòine taibhseach

eerie moss

leave behind the blessing of cnoc chalmac

malcolm's hillock

Breunalach was the stinking land, but named for what?
Cruaidh-Leac, Loinn-na-Biorag, and Cladhan are from
Richard Perry's memoir of Glen Feshie. Allt Ghealain rises
on The Maim and flows into the Dhé, east of Crathie. Allt
an Beal rises on Càrn Damhaireach, *the rut cairn*, and
flows into Allt Cristie Beag; Alexander says that broom
related names appear so frequently because it was
important for thatch and fodder. Am Beitheachann, which
Watson gives as *the little birch place*, flows into the Quoich
Water; this is now a fir wood and presumably birch were
the pioneer species. Cnoc Chalmac is dedicated to St Colm.
Canup is from the Gaelic, A' Chairbh, *the bent ridge* (of a
girth-saddle). Watson thinks that Drumargettie was named
for silver, ie money, rather than pale grass. No one now
knows why Mòine Taibhseach was named *the ghostly
peat-moss*. Tom Chluig is north-west of Bridge of Gairn.

Let Truth Tell Itself

Jim Carruth

Eating is an agricultural act
WENDELL BERRY

Never will you live the heft and carry,
the day's endless burden of bale and bale,
or sense the gravity and grip of every string.

Never will you feel the blistered hands,
the tightened chest, the aching spine,
the midday burn on shoulder and back.

Never will you hear those big engines turn
as they shudder the earth beneath your feet,
the incessant rhythm of combine and baler.

Never will you breathe in cut straw and diesel;
never will your raw throat choke on barley seed;
never will your eyes sting blind with sweat.

Never will you bend with workers in the field nor
share the harvest hurt of those who fill your table.

Biography of a Cow

Russell Jones

The cow lies
placid as the grass,
coal and cloud,
milk-heavy, calfless.

Milkers roll nipples
between their fingers,
fill the empty tanks white.
In the abattoir, others beef,
mop-handed. They strip
the cow from the cow.

You are a cow. Check
the health of your hoof, swish
your tail like a metronome
to keep ultimate time.

Rub at the years, forget the fields
of pyres and chemical walkthroughs. Pop
the lid of a lasagne. Pour a tumbler
of semi-skimmed. Calcify. The cow
pushes the grass against its stomach
and anticipates the storm.

Summerisle

Hugh McMillan

'Dog shite and plenty af it.'
Big Tem is talking of his cucumbers,
great phalluses,
thick and rubbered enough
to crack your head.
'The carrots dinnae like it,
they prefer human keech.'

What luck to be born here
in this verdant space,
though our cottages slip into the sea
and we are a place
for ghosts and shotguns
and fine views of the cosmos

uncluttered by street light
because our streets are empty,
only the regeneration offices open,
winking long into the diamond night.
In Spring the auld heids
will stamp around the maypole,
their caps cocked at the breeze
and we will count the missing:

our children gone
over the hills like fairies,
their replacements grim changelings
with water for blood
The Daily Telegraph for a newspaper,
and not enough shite for a carrot,
if they tried all year.

Breath of the Treemen

Matthew Macdonald

They wake
slowly,
gasps of life
escaping
breaks in the bark
sap tongues
licking away
fallen leaves.

They hate autumn
preferring the stability
of broad green leaves to
the variegation of
red, crimson, orange,
yellow, brown, copper.
The treemen have only
one word for autumn leaves:
dead

They breathe out
the heart of the forest
letting it rise
into the sunlight.
It is their offering
to a fierce god who
blesses and burns
with one hand.
They pray pine needles
to the sleepy god.

The only water
is the river
and it nourishes.

They do not see men
who move too fast
far too noisily
to be worth attention,
it is not hard
for them to hide;
small white eyes see
only what is expected
never what is in dreams,
they have forgotten
why iron was so treasured
why cream was left
for the hedgehogs
and why you never
let a rowan bleed.

They do not let
themselves be seen;
only heard in
day-weary branches
settling and creaking
in the forest.
Do not hunt for them

but watch
the morning prayer
of breathing.

The Town

Chris Boyland

They closed the
town today, took
the houses down in
sections, rolled our
gardens up like
carpets, loaded
them onto lorries
and we never
saw them again.

They packed all
our things in
boxes, labelled
children like parcels,
helped us onto the
railway specials
and took us all away.

Now, we lie down
in strange beds,
wearing clothes
that don't fit,
trying to fill
the empty shoes
of all the men
who never came home.

To Mohammed

Henry Bell

They arrested your brother today,
your youngest brother.
I remember you telling me
how the doctors come and the interrogators come
and they are all the same people
making sure not to break your body, but to bend it just enough.
You snapped a fag and poured the tobacco out on the table
as you said it. Just three of us in the Calton Bar after Hogmanay.
We'd walked up the Gallowgate and I was cold
and struggling through a hangover. How to write
when I think of you in a cell since Easter,
or drinking Buckfast in Palestine, laughing at my haircut.
You said everyone must resist in their own way.
'We cannot all be artists, we cannot all be fighters,
but the man that sweeps the street, he is resisting too.'

And the man who sits in prison.

Divali in Kessock

Arun Sood

We exchanged red threads
and looked for tiny dolphins
encircled in binoculars
on a finite weekend
with our father

whose torn diaries, journals
and spills across the carpet
sowed a bitter domesticity
sweetened briefly by the *mithai*
in your ornate red palms.

In the evening, *masala chai*
on a cold doorstep where
we shivered to watch fireworks
spray colours across the Forth
before dark, a lustred memory.

Autumn in Texas

Nancy Somerville

After the wedding
heading north on 281,
our windscreen is spattered
by what I think are autumn leaves
but my son's new wife tells me
it's clouds of Monarch butterflies
we're driving through
for miles.
It happens every year, she says;
two billion in a long haul flutter
escaping Canada's cold front.

The survivors will make it
to Mexico and hibernation
sheltered under the canopy
of the Sierra Madre,
clustered on branches,
the foliage of winter.

Come Spring
they'll fall from the trees,
search out mates
and carry north
the seeds of future generations
and I wonder if I'll have grandchildren
and if the butterflies will still be there
for them to see.

Squaring the circle

Finola Scott

They promise polar bears.
For days we head up, beyond
the tree line, to the white of the globe,
to abandoned sledges and flags.

In constant light we haunt the rails,
whales cruise past spouting careless,
but no polar bears. The ice field's not
where it should be. Its melting edge slips
in summer's heat. Sapphire glaciers shift
and retreat. Icebergs, the size of factories,
calve. The captain's map dissolves.

So this crystal morning, tannoys haul
dreamers from cabin to empty deck,
hard-core naturalists separate from tourists.
The dedicated don't pause to dress.
Held in the curve of the Arctic, pyjamas
peek from cosy coats and cardies.
Longitude and latitude slices of pie.

We scan bobbing floes and remember
ice-cream floats in cafes. Then walrus!
Blancmange blobs heave out of water, lumber,
roar and snort. Mothers loll, blubbery
babies big as cows practise skidding.
They slide and wobble on aquamarine, alert
for hunters. Tusks fear scrimshaw.

Cruising the Russian coast, we watch clouds
form over Murmansk. Industry sends smoke
signals over turquoise. Off the Scottish coast
scallops taste acid in their sea.

Lochlannach

Calum L MacLeòid

Ghabh mi comhairle na feannaige.
Thàinig mi air druim uilebheist.
Cha do chuir achadh nam muc-mara bacadh orm.
Dheasaich mi teicneòlas is fìor iarann.
Dh'fhàs mo chalpannan fuilteach.
Leasaich mi laghan iomchaidh.
Rinn mi iolairean à gealtairean.
Theasaich mi mac-meanmainn
Le taisbeanadh dathach ùr.
'S ann aca a bha an taghadh fad an t-siubhail
Is far an robh daoine tartmhor
Dh'òl iad.

Aon là
Bidh ainmean cèine aca orm
Càinidh daoine chràbhach mi
Ach fada às dèidh dhomh a bhith siubhal
Agus iad a' fuireachd gu dòigheil
Agus iad a' fuireachd gu sìtheil
Agus iad a' fuireachd gu cùramach
Lìonaidh fhathast ìomhaigh
Mo chairbh chaithte leònte
An cridhean glasa le miann feòla.

Thin Ice

John Bolland

For Marc Cornelissen and Philip De Roo, missing presumed drowned 200km south of Bathurst Island in the Canadian Arctic, 29 April 2015

We circled for an age to no avail.
The place they were, their 'there', was not.
The sea was flecked with broken pack.
The melting ice heaved, shattered on the swell.

The place they were, their 'there', was not.
The origin of their last signal – lost.
The melting ice heaved, shattered on the swell.
One sled dog stranded. Gear. No other trace.

The origin of their last signal lost
on the rising curve of warming currents.
One sled dog stranded. Gear. No other trace.
Only the ocean clenching like a fist.

Before the rising curve of warming currents
the ice recedes a little more each Spring.
The ocean clenches like a fist,
pumped full of energy and chaos.

The ice recedes a little more each Spring.
The place they were, their 'there' is not.
The ocean's full of energy and chaos.
Its patterns shift and circulations stall.

The place we are, our here – it may not be.
We know the risks but cannot know the hour.
The patterns shift and circulations stall
and we arrive and circle.

We know the risks but cannot know the hour.
The question's huge and simple as the ocean's flux.
Yet we arrive, and circle, wondering –
fuel burning in our engines like a fuse.

The question's simple as the ocean's flux.
Where will we be if all the ice is lost?
Fuel burning in our engines like a fuse,
we circle for an age to no avail.

The Sweet Science

Ross Wilson

Words lost the commentators
in thought fogs they thought were clear
but were not – anything but.
In this confused mist of things in conflict
lines are scored between eyes
like the lines old pugilists had to toe.
Now two girls approach that old scratch,
and an uncomfortable itch
has two former boxers search
for words to describe what's happening
right in front of them:
a woman punches a woman,
the hit strikes back,
and on it goes, and on,
until blood drips from cuts torn
and braided hair soaks sweat flowing.
And then, as if it were two men,
the commentators relax into it, talking
technique, tactics, until
some objection within
derails objectivity again,
and one of them says it, as if in pain:
not for me, women boxing.

It takes me back a decade or more
to an old boxer who swore:
the female body was not built to be hit.
And that was true, I remember thinking it,

before truth fogged over
like the eyes of a man hit
so hard his brain re-boots
as his boots wipe soles on air.

And a man's body was made for this?

Return

Finola Scott

*For the Chibok schoolgirls, kidnapped by Boko Haram,
April 2014*

Doubled by her child
your child spoiled
shop soiled sex
machined for soul-
less soldiers invaded
knocked up battered
your child hangs
between girl and
mother you force
anger down cradle
her and hers.

You hear but
can't listen. Bones
of bruised face
the same eyes
and not look inwards
hooded not knowing
her future not
wanting that past
strung between there
and here somewhere
she remains.

Chioroscuro

Ross Wilson

I once stood alone in a room
with *The Beheading of St John
The Baptist*. Pictures that lead to it
were soft with the haloes
and angels of divine intervention.

A current flowed through this one,
a voltage from another age,
shocking me with a decapitation
the artist missed by hundreds of years,
I by hundreds more.

Yet I entered on time,
as viewers do every time, always in time
for the ever happening aftermath:
executioner poised, ready to cut
whatever holds body and head together

while a girl holds a platter
to remove one from the other, forever.
The main event interested me less
than two prisoners:
minor characters, like most of us,

staring, helpless, through the bars
of a window that could be
a picture frame or monitor
through which someone somewhere
watches today's version of events, online.

All the Verbs from Glasgow City Council's New Proposed Management Rules Regulating Public Parks, in Order, in Lower Case, Preserving Line Breaks and Inserting a Stanza Break for Each New Section, Followed by Every Word Containing 'No' in the Order They Appear, This Time in Upper Case: An Elegy

Harry Giles

regulating
referred conferred referred referred makes following

means is owned occupied managed is has is used connected
     foregoing include
means has undertaken carry out relating
means extending amending
means comprising is organised has had organised includes
     advertised operating messaging
means committed is cause using
means authorised

shall
enter leave
enter remain closed
commit
enter authorised do
damage remove
leave provided
obstruct
carry discharge
bring deposit leave cause
smoke prohibiting

may refuse shall dispersed
may make exempting would include has believe used said
    result
congregates is cause is empowered take ensure is dispersed
    may include taking seeking required
is is suffered occasioned take suffered was

allowed is posted must be kept is is respond is kept
ensure is picked removed deposited
shall
exercise
displace disturb ill-treat injure take destroy
set use taking

canoeing rafting rowing sailing swimming are managed
dipping is taken should be returned
shall
dam obstruct
take catch injure destroy disturb fishing
pollute
shall go formed intimating is do is displayed

71

entering leaving designated transporting require

permitted must be driven must obstruct risk causing must
exceed

parking provided provided are are being used are parking
reserves impose parking

parking is allowed

abandoned parked parked designated parking parked
foregoing causing removed stored displayed

cycling
cycling designated
must maintain ensure do endanger should exceed

shall
camp
light
are allowed provided is paid must be removed

be sold supplied granted
consumed prohibiting designated
is shall enter remain

shall agreeing comply issued
organise take part
display distribute advertising
organise participate betting gaming
recruit drill practice
use controlled
play practice
play practice
leave
make landing
shall
use play indicating

solicit collect
use is is detecting is issued detecting detecting
geocaching is allowed geocaching is followed
shall operate play play amplified

shall
enter reserved use accompanied assisted using
erect
erect affix
erect attach entitled remove shall pay
dispose cremated deceased
hang beat shake sweep brush cleanse

shall
sell hire
carry
beg solicit
shall include are limited following
walking
training make use
seeking use care
guided made
is

reserves levy use provided shall alter
is required use use designated growing may levy use

has believing contravened contravening contravene
    foregoing expel exclude
contravenes attempts contravene foregoing is contravene
    made exceeding
is expelled excluded fails leave re-enters shall be

NOT NOT ANNOYANCE NOMINEE NO ONE NOT
NOTICE NOT NOT NOTICE NO ONE CANOEING
NO ONE NO ONE NOTICE NOT NOT NOT NOT
NOT NO ONE CANNOT CANNOT NO ONE NO
NOTICE NO NOTICE NO NO ONE NOTICE NOTICE
NOTICE NO ONE NOT NOTICE NOT

The Chair

Chris Boyland

We came to bury the chair today.
There weren't that many of us,
a small group of friends
and a gaggle of gossipy ladies,
who sat at the back and talked happily
about funerals and the price of steak mince.

They carried the chair down the aisle,
black crepe ribbons tied to its armrests,
vinyl cushions polished to a shine.
Everyone thought it looked so nice,
with its new rubber tyres and gleaming spokes.

The priest gave a eulogy for the chair.
How it had spent its days in the service of others,
tirelessly (if you'll excuse the pun),
ever ready to bear its load, to follow its path
towards some higher purpose, blessed by God.

After the service, they took the chair away.
We went to eat sandwiches and drink tea,
and someone mentioned, as a passing thought,
this little girl who'd sat in the chair and
gone around in it, wherever it went.
But no-one could recall her face or,
when we thought about it, who she was
or even if she'd really been there at all.

Solidarity

William Bonar

Lik the puir huis in here, the day, she said,
no even a biscuit. The tea lady,
luikin aulder than her years in thon ugsome green
domestics huvtae wear, in case emdy mistakes thaim
fur sumdy important, is pit oot.

When she huz thaim, she pits doon a Rich Tea
lik a talisman aside the plastic cup.
A haily wafer, sister tae brither,
the diffrince atween enough an waant.
Aye, hard times, I say, only hauf-kiddin.

Hid

Nancy Somerville

It's about oxters and pinkies
and all the other words underlined in red
when you type them in,
even though they've always been here.

It's about aye, and naw and mibbe,
and the red line's there now
an Ah'm seein rid.
Keep the heid,
an therr it is agane,
ma mither tongue, reduced tae a mistake
lik it's no real, no valid.
Do you mean head?

Naw Ah don't, Ah mean heid,
an a the ither wurds that get a rid unnerline
an it keeps wantin (*Do you mean wanton?*)
tae chynge it tae *hid*
which is ironic, is it no?

Scottish Election Tongue Twister *or* A Phrase That is Designed to be Difficult to Articulate Properly

Henry Bell

red tory yellow tory red tory yellow tory red tory yellow tory
red tory yellow tory red tory yellow tory red tory yellow tory
red tory yellow tory red tory yellow tory red tory yellow tory
red tory yellow tory red tory yellow tory red tory yellow tory
red tory yellow tory red tory yellow tory red tory yellow tory
red tory yellow tory red tory yellow tory red tory yellow tory
red tory yellow tory red tory yellow tory red tory yellow tory
red tory yellow tory red tory yellow tory red tory yellow tory
red tory yellow tory red tory yellow tory red tory yellow tory
red tory yellow tory red tory yellow tory red tory yellow tory
red tory yellow tory red tory yellow tory red tory yellow tory
red tory yellow tory red tory yellow tory green tory yellow
tory red tory yellow tory red tory yellow tory red tory yellow
tory red tory yellow tory red tory yellow tory blue tory
yellow tory red tory yellow tory red tory yellow tory red tory
yellow tory red tory yellow tory red tory yellow tory red tory
yellow tory red tory yellow tory red tory yellow tory red tory
yellow tory red tory yellow tory red tory yellow tory red tory
yellow tory red tory yellow tory red tory yellow tory red tory
yellow tory red tory yellow tory red tory yellow tory red tory
yellow tory red tory yellow tory red tory yellow tory red tory
yellow tory red tory yellow tory red tory yellow tory red tory
yellow tory red tory yellow tory red tory yellow tory red tory
yellow tory red tory yellow tory red tory yellow tory red tory
yellow tory red tory yellow tory red tory yellow tory red tory

The Exceptionals

David Forrest

We are the unco, byous, braw exceptionals!
Push it intae words
bang it doon tae the table In Inglis
this is ma hert, this is ma heid
Whack: Ah'm fae Glesga. Aye! Aye! Aye!

Claimed it, cherished it, chanted it, aye.
Never really earnt it but.
Never really looked at it in a mirror.
Never really mended it, missed it
jis cherished it, kissed it.

This is who we are so haud ontae it – the mauments we
were guid, see that, see that, that's Scotland, aye, that's us.
Miners. Inventors. Poleteecians. That's us. Clearances, aye.
That's us too. Hume. David Hume. That's us... och, it's
gone again, but did you see it there, aye? Aye.

Get it awa fae ye the mauments we were hertless, racist,
cruel, the mauments we didna care, the mauments we
looked awa an ravaged your country bare. Aye. Aye. A
poke in the 'aye'.
Oor history's blue and white wi no blood red!
Oor country's sober, fat, unfed!
We are the unco, byous, braw exceptionals!
Repeat it, believe it, repeat it, believe it
it wisna me
Repeat it. Believe it.
It wisna me, it wisna me!

See, it wis aw ae us, cept when it wisna.
Close the curtains. Open the blogs. Let the guid stuff in.
Mebbe Scotland's mair than whit ye think it is
and at the same time? Mebbe Scotland's less.
Close the blogs. Open the curtains. Let the guid stuff in.

Ower muckle poetry oan wan wird politeecs
no jis aye or naw but ane an aw
the kick, the blaw
dinna say your fir us or agin us
we ken wir baith saunts an sinners.

A Voter's Reflections in Rhyme

Calum Rodger

Written on the morning of 18 September 2014.

'Should Scotland be an independent country?'
To be honest I wanted so much more
I don't need Rabbie Burns, but they ask me so abruptly
And 'yes' or 'no' don't lend themselves to metaphor.

Then there's the trek to the community centre
With its wee metal boxes and flimsy stalls
Some auld yin at the desk, pencil and paper
The tech, the venue, the staff – a bit rustic, that's all.

But I have never been a fraction as excited
At Caesura, the Sub Club or Yellowcraigs beach
As when making that mark – as if something ignited –
A spark that turned talk into serious speech

I knew I'd be buzzing, but something surprised
Beyond all the novelty and singular thrill
It started as a feeling, and then crystallised:
The graphite was etching my political will

A strange new electric, an unfamiliar frisson
A vote not felt to be futile and bored
I heard my own voice, and heard all who listened
Speech is only serious when it's heard

'Should Scotland be an independent country?'
Ask this question 4.289 million times
And listen as a million pencils bluntly
Change everything with two bisecting lines.

Postscript

Written on the evening of 18 September 2014

What beautiful platitudes, but here comes the postscript
I'm drunk – the sentimental stage has passed
This stanza's slightly different – the BBC would have to cut it
Basically, yous better all be voting YAS

For when today tick-tocks into tomorrow
And the eagle comes swooping through the glen
If the winner is the one that's filled with sorrow
You know the one, the one that starts with 'n'
I'll probably cry and never vote again
I'll probably cry, and never vote again.

And So the People Spoke 18–9–2014

Anita John

A year like no other when the cuckoo circled the sheep field,
delivered the hottest of summers with its cry;
when blackthorn hung heavy with star-burst
and flies shimmered above the waters of the Tweed,
their first and last dance;

when the politician's voice foretold
of a once-in-a-lifetime, irreversible choice,
and people twittered and tweeted;
when opinions might be changed
by the counting out of daisy petals;

when the nation rode high as an osprey
over wind turbine and mountain;
when 'Yes' signs appeared
on windows and walls,
'No' signs in wide-open fields;

when swallows nested for the first time in our garden shed
and we saw the blue-jay wings of the magpie:
a golden green glimmering;
when the land-line yammered for our *first time voter*,
and hares jinked and janked down the Kitleyknowe Road;

when the sun sparked off slate each morning;
when Edinburgh cupcakes sold in their thousands:
the Saltire, the Union Jack and the Don't Knows;
when change was a salt taste in the wind
and temperatures rose to 30 degrees;

when the eyes of Europe followed like a hawk;
when three weeks stretched like a lifetime;
when four million people took to the streets;
when Scotland cast its vote.

Searmonaiche Tadhalach

Greg MacThòmais

Tha mi ag ùrnaigh mas fhìor fo do chrannag
Ag aomadh mo chinn ach sùilean fosgailte farsaing
Guth air choireigin a' guidhe gun can thu nì mì-chneasta
A bheir air an t-aithreachan a-rithist fàgail
Nitheigin mu bheatha shaoghalta ar latha-ne
Bhon eòlas aig fear dùinte liath
Air casg-breith no ministearan gèidh
Gun deachaidh a h-uile sgath bhuaithe
Nuair a chaill sinn ar n-anam clèireach
Na linntean geala
Nuair a dh'aoradh bean do mhòrachd a duine pòsta
Nuair a riaghladh do leithid-sa paraiste le làmh làidir an
    tighearna.
Ach tha thu sèimh nad bheachdan an-diugh, a shearmonaiche
A-mach air sgriobtar a tha, cha mhòr, sòisealach
Mu dhìon nam bochd is sgaoileadh a' bheairteis
A tha còrdadh rium math gu leòr
An turas seo
Oir nach tuirteadh am badeigin gur beannaichte sibhse a
    tha bochd?

Highland Disunion

Arun Sood

When Morag met Vishal
Papa did not protest but
welcomed the Hindu doctor
who liked a dram and once
danced bhangra atop the
pool table in Strontian Hotel,

But when Ina eloped with Hugh
the handsome Catholic marine
bottles splintered floorboards
lest, he, frowning Donald-John,
would ever bless a fenian-spouse
for Highland reasons he knew well, perhaps.

Morag, ushered in white satin
towards a cross and kind man
she could never worship, met eyes
with Ina alone in the aisle that day:
when they both cursed the Gods
that sanctioned their disunion.

Dealachadh Gàidhealach

Arun Sood
Translation of 'Highland Disunion' by Calum L MacLeòid

Nuair a choinnich Morag ri Vishal
cha do thog Boban fianais ach
chuir e fàilte air an dotair Hionduthach
a ghabhadh drama agus a dhanns
bhangra uair air mullach bòrd-cluiche
an Taigh-òsta sta Sròn an t-Sìthein,
Ach nuair a theich Ina le Ùisdean
an saighdear grinn Caitligeach
sgealb botail clàran-ùrlair
air eagal is gum beannaicheadh, esan,
Dòmhnall Iain nan gruaim, papanach de chèile
a thoradh adhbharan Gàidhealach
air an robh e eòlach gu leòr, 's dòcha.
Nuair a chunnaic Morag, stiùirichte na sìoda geal
a dh'ionnsaigh crann-cheusta is fir laghach
dhan nach dèanadh i adhradh,
Ina na h-aonar anns an trannsa an latha ud:
chuir iad mallachd air na Diathan
a cheadaich an dealachadh.

Crossing the Road

Gavin Cameron

AC/DC, binary,
yin and yang, fence-sitter.
Neither fish nor fowl,
diet poof, switch-hitter.
Comme ci, comme ça,
does anything that moves.
Plays for both teams,
ambisextrous, coitally confused.
Flip-flopper, in denial,
going through a phase.
Half-rice, half-chips,
Arthur/Martha, Tommy Two-Ways.
Not sort of straight, not sort of gay,
the word you can't appear to say:
bisexual.

Alice Coy Told Me How

Henry Bell

The world narrowed to a single point.
The war, the wars, a single point.
The Iraq Palestine Gaza sexism occupation
all that blurred to nothing.

'My back is broken.' The last words Rachel Corrie ever said.
I dropped my phone
took her head in my hands to stabilise her spine.
Nearby the bulldozers and tanks were driving.
The land scraped clean of homes, to a steel wall.

The world, my world, narrowed to just four people.
I held Rachel's head.
On her right and left Greg and Will knelt beside her,
three friends told her we loved her
how awesome she was
that she was going to be ok.

I observed the thin skin around her eyes and ears
blackening with blood
from the bleeding in her brain.
At that moment there were just four of us in the world,
And one was dying as we held her.
This is the detail in every statistic:

a world narrowed in.
People holding their loved ones

their soft flesh

the metals of war

For Refuge

Pippa Little

Use no names. Roads
have been whited out,
redacted. Hone your oldest sense.
Learn the wind,
memorise where it goes
bearing your odours. The truck-stops
are roofless churches.
Comma-birds on power lines
swollen by rain
fall away.
Comfort yourself,
there will be stars in the dark
travelling towards you,
smaller and smaller.

Trust the earth
with your bandaged feet,
the pockets sewn shut by your mother.
Carry only such things
as snowflakes, eyelashes,
for the future may not make you out.

Slack Water

Marjorie Lofti Gill

i   Mediterranean

Its waters are a checkpoint,
    the crease of folded news,
the rope's midway mark
    in a game of tug of war.
Dredge the bottom
    for the only colour
in this graveyard of sea;
    from here, its surface
is as smooth as the skin
    stretching the palm
of your hand, or that old
    warped mirror, the one
that says you are
    the fairest in the land.

ii   Rescue

If bedrock can break apart,
     leave its offspring
resting in the limbs
     of tenant trees,
then I can hand my child
     to the strange man in white
on the other boat, the one
     who offers me the trunks
of his forearms, asks me
     to hold out this part
of myself, the child, who even now,
     suspended midair
between vessels, pleads
     with me to stay.

iii   Mohammed says *

you forget   Europe

you forget   Tunisia

you forget   Libya

you forget   everything

you think
        I will die

this question
            (watch
                left   right
                up   down

        only blue sky   blue water   strong waves
        the boat   it's full of water)

    ask the driver to tell us

        if the weather stay   *we'll be fine*
        if the weather windy   *I say I'm sorry*

            (see yourself   so little   in this vast sea)

    why this dangerous adventure
                            (it's not adventure)

we   are   fine   now

we   are   fine

but   I   not

                         must
                         forget

* Words taken from an interview with a Tunisian refugee on *The Guardian* website.

iv Lament

After the tongue latch clicks
into place, and the key grinds
full circle, what is the sound
in the room? (We're never alone
with our voices.) When the engine fails
to keep the beat, there's only the tug
of gravity and the steady pull
of bottom; even the seawater slapping
the deck is lost to fists at the door.
Soon the weave of limbs is a tangle
of telephone wires, though no operator
listens to the refrain of pleas, please,
or counts the bargains gone wrong.
Babies' cries become birdsong,
a language we've forgotten,
and the others go quiet, slip like slates
into the sea, their pockets filled
with worry, beads clattering
against one another, glassy eyes
still waiting to be fingered.

v   Fisherman

It's our code to go when called,
though now we are fishers of men,
and three days later, after the laws
of chemistry and biology take hold,
we become fishers of bloated bodies
floating like the bloom of lilies
at dusk across the water's surface.
Someday, the sheer number locked
into its hull will lift a boat to surface,
will raise the scraps of wood and metal
that first weighted them down; we'll find
the ghost ship floating, hull skyward
like the soft underside of a whale.

Arcadia

Rona Fitzgerald

On the sea there was ease, waves soothed
fears receded. The children loved the rhythm,
enthralled as silver fish dart under aquamarine.

Then the endless blue of the Greek coast,
a place of heroes, culture, democracy.
And safety. Europe will look after us.

Poetry Reading, Edinburgh, 1960

Stewart Sanderson

So much is written in a photograph:
a criticism, I would say, of life
that something stolen from experience
for one moment can hold more of the dance
we have inherited than simply being
a part of it. There is a roch wind straying
through this picture of a thin young man
reading his poem out. I count fifteen
around him, some cross-legged on the floor
while others stand. A few have bagged a chair.
Together they make up a ring of pale
half-century-old faces. For a while
I've wondered what became of each of them
after the reading finished. Heading home
over the Meadows, up the Canongate
or down Leith Walk, they vanish in the night
of fifty years ago, leaving no trace
save this one, of their brief togetherness
in somebody's front room. Frozen mid-word
the poet's mouth hangs open. Pre-prepared
preamble done, he lets the made thing go
as is the only decent thing to do
with any language loved; with syntax shaped
and knapped until a larger meaning slipped
in at the edges of the utterance.

A very civil disobedience
you might think, but there is rebellion
in this: the gilded youth of Duddingston,
Marchmont and Musselburgh, gathered to hear
a poem carry on the smoky air
while what could well be cigarettes go round
passed like penny sweets from hand to hand.
The Scottish revolution won't begin
for quite some time (to date nobody's seen
the late train sweeping into Waverley
depositing a bearded émigré
and new world on the platform). Nonetheless
there is, perhaps, a growing sense of place
in these young people's thoughts: a subtle thing
returning as a half-remembered song
will to the ear whenever certain chords
tremble in concert. At their best, the words
a poet lives by have some part to play
mapping this delicate geography
of feeling; teaching us to bear our loss
with what I'd hesitantly label grace.

Afterword

Robert Crawford

Bardic Voice

A lecture delivered at the National Library of Scotland on 23 September 2015 as part of the Poetic Politics *conference, marking the first anniversary of the Scottish Independence Referendum. A version of this lecture also appeared in the journal* Irish Pages Vol. 9 No. 1 *in 2015.*

NO POET SHOULD feel obliged to engage with politics. All poets should be free to do so. A poet who wants to write politically hears two voices. One, the bardic voice, urges him or her to speak on behalf of a community, a tribe, a gender, a nation; the other insists only on truth to the individual self, an unstable self which may elude communal, tribal, gender or national definition. In Scotland, as in Ireland, and many other countries, bardic voice is a strong presence (even in fiction). It's clearly there in Gaelic poetry. When Lachlann Mór MacMhuirich (here in my translation) incites his clansmen,

> Be belters, be brandishers,
> Be bonny, be batterers

he's speaking to and for the tribe. Inflected differently, that bardic impulse is there in the public poetry of that Gaelic-speaking Latinist George Buchanan whose Renaissance Latin epithalamium for the marriage of Mary Queen of Scots to the French Dauphin includes a paean to Scotland in which Buchanan operates as a proto-poet laureate. In

Scots and English, our starriest bard is Burns – 'Caledonia's Bard, brother Burns', as he was called masonically in this city. Signing himself 'Yours for Scotland' and identifying with the heart-breaking 'Little White Rose', Hugh MacDiarmid, too, like Sorley MacLean, sought out a bardic role, which was for him at times, as it had been on occasion for Burns, a political one.

Yet there are other great Scottish poets for whom this bardic voice has been something to eschew, or at least to modify vigorously; William Dunbar can deploy bardic voice, including stinging, satirical bardic voice (for surely flyting is the flipside of bardic encomium), but in that phrase 'Ersche brybour baird', the word 'baird' (bard) is a Lowland insult; in his 'Lament for the Makaris', Dunbar's truest tribe is simply the poets, and not absolutely all those makars in that poem are Scottish; William Drummond of Hawthornden, the first Scottish poet to write English with complete fluency, was more of a recluse than a bard in his faction-ridden land. More recently, Norman MacCaig seemed eager to renounce the bardic in one of his most political poems, 'Patriot', in which he declares slyly and with vehement individualism,

My only country
is six feet high
and whether I love it or not
I'll die
for its independence.

The quarrel with himself out of which Yeats made poetry was principally an argument between individual (often erotic) lyric voice and bardic voice. There is a related quarrel within the poetries of Seamus Heaney, Eavan Boland, and many other recent Irish poets, including Paul

Muldoon, that most influential English-language poet of his generation. The phrase 'bardic voice' sounds old-fashioned; it seems to belong, perhaps, to medieval Gaelic chieftains or to that world of declamation set out by Catherine Robson, whose book *Heartbeats: Everyday Life and the Memorized Poem* (2012) centres on the 19th century and has on its cover a kilted schoolboy reciting Robert Burns. Maybe instead of using the term 'bardic voice', I should be referring to poetry that is fitted with its own effective public-address system, but I want to stick with the term 'bardic voice' not least because it emphasises the longevity of poetry as an archaic and abiding as well as a modern art form. 'Bardic voice' is a sound system, both because of the way it orders a system of sounds and because its sense of attunement or attack is an attempt to articulate, however indirectly, something of a sound system of government.

I admit that the phrase 'bardic voice' still makes us awkward here in the land of James Macpherson; it risks sounding too antique, too bound to the norms of Romantic lastness, too Ossianic. Yet the term 'bardic voice' is worth using because it signals not only poetry's access to the power of public address, but also since it reminds us how important such access has been in Scotland, Ireland, and elsewhere. Ironically, and perhaps whetted by their long residence in England, there may be more Scottish bardic voice in the English-based Scottish poets WN Herbert and Jackie Kay than in some of the best known Scottish-based poets of my generation. In their poetic practice John Burnside and Don Paterson have refused to bring bardic voice to issues of national identity and the politics of British unionism or Scottish independence. On rare occasions Kathleen Jamie (perhaps like Meg Bateman) has adopted bardic voice only to unshackle herself from it, whether in 'The Queen of Sheba' or in 'Mr and Mrs Scotland are Dead'.

Bardic voice can be a temptation, even an off-the-peg uniform, for Scottish poets. The temptation is grandiosity, egotism, and reductivism: the illusion that the nation and the self, the 'I', are pompously, even bumptiously, at one. I recognise that temptation; but I remain committed to risking at times elements of bardic voice. From my first collection of poems, *A Scottish Assembly*, in 1990, I've felt an attraction to the possibilities not just of so-called private voice but of kinds of bardic or public voice, of poetry that can articulate aspects of a national community with a subtle but unashamed political inflection. Like many – probably most – poets of my generation and the preceding generation, I lived outside Scotland for a considerable time in my 20s, and my decision to return here was an act of deliberate commitment. It was during six years in England, and not least as the result of a relationship with a refugee, that I came to realise what it meant to me to be Scottish and some of the things that being Scottish might mean in and for poetry. I chose for my first book an epigraph from Margaret Atwood:

> Some people think that the word Nationalism means 'let's all put on jackboots and kill everybody else', but our cultural nationalism has a very modest mandate – namely that we exist. It seems to threaten some people.

But, though *A Scottish Assembly* is by no means *all* political, its poems, like some of the poems in my more recent collections, go beyond mere cultural nationalism to point in the direction of political independence. Though my favourite poet remains TS Eliot (who once wrote that 'History is now and England') and my orientation is both instinctively and deliberately Scottish-international, my biography of Burns is clearly titled *The Bard*, and I do believe in the possibilities for Scottish poets of a bardic stance, but not a simplistic one. Much of what I've written in poetry and in prose has been geared to articulating a sense of Scottish identities as complex and of our poetic traditions as multiple. Hence the title of the early 1990s magazine *Scotlands*, and the design of the *Penguin Book of Scottish Verse* which Mick Imlah and I edited and which begins with that Latin masterwork the 'Altus Prosator' along with my old teacher Edwin Morgan's striking facing translation. Hence the resolutely polylingual argument to my history of Scottish literature, *Scotland's Books*; and when I say resolutely polylingual, I don't mean simply the mantra of English, Scots, and Gaelic; I mean also Latin, Old English, Old French, Old Norse, Old Welsh, as well as more recent immigrant tongues: the whole hybrid and gloriously impure caboodle.

I admire the way that Morgan for Scots and English, and more recently Meg Bateman for Gaelic, have acted not just as poet but also as warden and sharer of the hoard – anthologizing, criticising, writing literary history, and translating the poetry of the past without compromising the creative gift. Bateman and Morgan have fused to a risky yet commendable extent the professorial and the bardic. Let me repeat that poets don't have to speak for the nation, the gender, the sexual orientation, the tribe, but they can try at times to do so; and at times such as the 2014 independence referendum, I think that (though I do understand why some of the poets I've mentioned resisted doing so in their work) bardic voice – whether it was Liz Lochhead channelling Burns in the Portrait Gallery or young poets reading in village halls – was often the appropriate thing to risk.

Perhaps now, though, in the period after our independence referendum we've become even more wary of yoking – as some of us did during the political campaign – poetry and politics. And, yes, in the decades since the heyday of Hugh MacDiarmid, many have argued that the two should be kept apart. In 2014 I published a sequence of political poems that were part of my collection, *Testament,* and also a prose book: *Bannockburns: Scottish Independence and Literary Imagination, 1314–2014.* Neither of these books is simply propagandistic. Yet it would be hard to read either without realising that I support Scottish independence. In the immediate aftermath of the 2014 independence referendum it was hard not to feel a shiver of failure. Whatever poets did to back 'the cause', it was not enough. All those readings, those would-be bardic songs, those discussions, those attempts to sing a new Scotland into being, were almost, but not quite, enough.

It wisnae us, of course. It was the economists, the politicians, the rest. They didn't quite get their act together. The months after the Scottish independence referendum, for those among the 45 per cent at least, were months of 'if only'. If only there had been a six per cent swing in the right direction. If only the currency question had been more deftly addressed. If only culture had been debated as much as oil. Yet, let's face it, O fellow bookish ones here in the National Library, nobody really issues the lament, 'If only there had been some better sonnets.' Poetry, WH Auden so famously said in his elegy for WB Yeats, 'makes nothing happen'.

Yeats didn't seem to believe that, though. When, close to the end of his life, his poem 'The Man and the Echo' posed the question, 'Did that play of mine send out / Certain men the English shot?' the implied answer is not entirely clear, but the anxiety that poetry does indeed have the power to make things happen is evident. In his book *Poetry, Poets, Readers: Making Things Happen* (2002) the English poet and critic Peter Robinson has devoted much intellectual energy to the issue of whether or not poetry makes things happen, and it's a question that poets and readers – including those in Scotland now – shouldn't shirk. Scotland is neither Ireland, nor America; to start with, it is one of the unusual glories of modern Scottish nationalism that no man, nor woman, nor child has been shot as a result of it. Yet we can and do learn from aligning ourselves with Irish, American, Australian, and other poetries. In her book *Songs of Ourselves: The Uses of Poetry in America* (2007) the historian Joan Shelley Rubin shows how one of the jobs American poetry has done is to say, 'I Am an American'. Yeats – some of whose finest poems clearly and conflictedly say 'I Am Irish' – gives the lie to any assertion that poetry cannot or should not be political and cannot take on a bardic, national voice with aplomb. Yet Yeats also vigorously asserts the poet's impulse to cut away from the political, and follow the (sometimes lustful) lyric impulse. His late poem 'Politics' begins:

> How can I, that girl standing there,
> My attention fix
> On Roman or on Russian
> Or on Spanish politics?

and this poem concludes with the simple, and lamenting exclamation,

> But O that I were young again
> And held her in my arms!

I salute Yeats's wandering eye: there is poetry in it as there was in his hopeless, intrepid pursuit of Maud Gonne decades earlier. But I honour, too, his continuing engagement, however difficult, with politics; and I think we should go on reflecting on that here in contemporary Edinburgh.

For if Yeats is emblematic of the great political poet, then he is also an emblem of long and sometimes anguished bardic waiting, and waiting is certainly the situation in which we find ourselves in today's Scotland. No sooner was our referendum narrowly lost – a swing of six per cent would have made all the difference – than it seemed that in the most recent UK general election that the cause of Scottish independence, as if on the rebound, was on a winning streak. For those of us who want to see an independent Scotland, the issue now is how best to wait, how to endure waiting, and how to sustain that waiting.

Well, Yeats waited, and poetry is good at sustaining, at keeping open long lines of communication. Yeats, the poet of urgency, was also a great poet of committed resilience, his sustaining lines of communication running to Indian and Japanese and ancient Greek culture as well as to London, Oxford, Stone Cottage, Dublin, and Sligo. It was in the early 1890s, *three decades* before the founding of an Irish Free State, that he addressed himself 'To Ireland in the Coming Times' and wanted to be 'brother of a company' of distinctively Irish nationalist poets. It was over 20 years later that the 'terrible beauty' was 'born', and it was almost another 20 years before Yeats the parliamentary Senator would assert with regard to vague Utopianism that it could produce as 'An image of such politics' a 'withered old and skeleton-gaunt' humanity. Yeats is an inspiration: his resilient and lyrical waiting paid off; but Yeats is also a sounder of warnings against making the heart a stone – against poetry simply and solely as propaganda.

Poetry, including bardic poetry (and perhaps no

successful poetry is purely 'bardic' in the most reductive sense of that word) must be something subtler and more oblique than propaganda, while still asserting a public voice. Most of Yeats's poetry is not political, even if he could rise on key occasions to being a great political poet. Yeats's bardic example may be set beside Burns's bardic example as a magnificent instance of a poet who can be political without renouncing his gift. Burns's bardic humour is glorious, and sets him apart from Yeats, but Burns is also a serious political poet. The song that begins 'Scots wha hae' is clearly a song of Scottish independence, but also a song of the Enlightenment; it is attuned to the French Revolution as well as to Bannockburn. Yet most of Burns's work is not so directly political. The bulk of MacDiarmid's best poems are not political either, or at least not narrowly political. And the same goes for Neruda, and for Seferis, that poet-translator-diplomat true not just to the Greek past but also to the uncanny and universal 'secrets of the sea' that are 'forgotten on the shore'. Who in their right mind would choose to represent MacDiarmid by one of the Hymns to Lenin rather than by 'Empty Vessel' or 'The Bonnie Broukit Bairn'?

It's good to think here in the National Library about poetry and politics not just in the immediate arena but also in much wider contexts. Whatever else they need to be, all poets must, at times, be bookish; that is, they need to read deeply and love their art not just in their own country and community, but across space and time. That is what nourishes us. Poems need to live on the breath and in the moment, but they need, too, to be able to last, to move across boundaries of chronology and culture. Good poetry doesn't belong exclusively to one generation, either living or dead. Each of us, if we write verse, must find our own way of articulating that. Since the referendum I have been working on a series of poems asserting the resilient quidditas of Glasgow, Edinburgh, Greenock, Dundee, Aberdeen – poems of Scottish cities, but also on a book in Scots called *Chinese Makars*, where the poems have absolutely nothing to do with Scottish politics. I hope that to work like this, like writing about TS Eliot, is a way of keeping open those long lines of communication which poetry offers and which too narrow adherence to any 'party line' of political cause can threaten to atrophy. Whatever else it is, the present is a time to assert and reassert internationalism in this country; which need not mean forgetting about locality or independence.

One of the most arresting questions asked about art and the referendum came from our greatest composer, James MacMillan, when he asked where was the great art that came out of all the referendum Yes campaigning? You can bounce the question back, of course: what was the great art of No? Yet instead of doing that, and just to induce even more cultural anxiety, one might ask, where is the great art that's appeared *since* the referendum vote? But to think that way is misguided. Again, it's important to stand back and take a wider perspective. In terms of Scottish poetry, it does seem hard to ignore that so many of the poets of recent times from MacDiarmid and MacCaig to Lochhead and Jamie have been supporters of independence; yet, though it may be valid to do so at certain times, there are dangers in looking at their work or public pronouncements *only* in search of political commitment. To do so may be valid but sort-sighted. If we take a longer, larger view of the politics of poetry, then what is more striking is the absence of support for British unionism in modern poetry from these islands. It is as easy to find great poetry that articulates a sense of England ('History is now and England') in the poetry of the last century as it is to locate poetry that attempts (often successfully) to articulate kinds of Scottishness or Irishness; yet the poetry of Britishness (as distinct from jingoistic verse) is very hard to find.

That fact tells its own story, and it is a story replicated in fiction. If you remove from literary history the powerful Scottish Unionist articulations of some supposed Britishness voiced in the 18th and 19th centuries by such novelist-poets as Smollett and Scott, then it is stunning how little articulation of Britishness there is in English fiction. No major English novel is set in Scotland, for instance, with the questionable exception of Woolf's *To the Lighthouse*, which may be nominally located on the Isle of Skye, but whose milieu smacks very much of the beautiful south-west English environment of Woolf's childhood summers. Ultimately, this failure to articulate positive ideals of Britishness is a striking aspect of literature from England, and, though 18th- and 19th-century Scottish writers attempted to remedy it by championing in 'Rule, Britannia' and elsewhere an ideal of a United Britain which included 'Caledonia stern and wild', it is hard to discern this British strain in Scottish literature beyond John Buchan. So, what I am arguing is that taking a wider-scale view of Scottish, English, and British literature strengthens, rather than in any sense compromises, the view that the auguries of writing in poetry as in fiction continue to point in the direction of Scottish independence. Taking such a view sustains our waiting.

We should not expect masterworks to appear every other Wednesday. We should not beat ourselves up unduly if even in 2014 no clear masterwork was published to articulate the dream of Scottish independence in poetry. Instead, while taking into account the textual evidence of such immediate productions as Christopher Silver's 2014 anthology *Inspired by Independence* (to which I, like many others, was delighted to contribute), we should realise too that such a book and other literary gatherings are part of a greater, carrying stream that certainly does include impressive individual works and bodies of writing from the recent and more distant past. Among these, surely, and now sifted by time, are the work of Alasdair Gray and Edwin Morgan; and, sustainingly, though Morgan died in 2010 and Gray is now seriously ill, recent months have brought significant signs that the work of each continues to inform and underpin debates about literary politics. In Gray's case David Greig's striking theatrical adaptation of *Lanark* now presents a stage version (made by an important dramatist vehement in his support for the Yes campaign in 2014) of the most famous novel by a Scottish novelist celebrated for his commitment to the cause of Scottish independence. While *Lanark* is certainly not the same book as Gray's *Why Scots Should Rule Scotland*, nonetheless, as I argue in *Bannockburns*, Gray's perennial theme of the individual who seeks independence from a situation of entrapment can be seen as having a political dimension, and one that persists in the context of today's Scotland.

For readers of Edwin Morgan, the publication of his large selected correspondence in *The Midnight Letterbox* serves to emphasise that most of Morgan's literary interests were *not* political. Indeed it can be amusing to see Morgan in 1968 wondering if people may react to a poet's politics simply in terms of 'Oh, I see old MacDiarmid's at it again... meaning that it is a sort of poet's privilege to be interested in politics but nevertheless to be fairly likely to be foolish.' Morgan was wary of the too narrowly 'Scottish', and though his imaginative fascination with metamorphosis does have a political dimension, one detects surprisingly little interest in Scottish politics in this particular selection of his letters, and what is there comes relatively late. In 1987 he writes how 'Alan Brownjohn of the Poetry Society in London is collecting poets' voting intentions, plus reasons for choice; I said SNP since I saw Scotland as "a frustrated republic and would like to help it to become a real one."' This is the Morgan who had published *Sonnets from Scotland* in 1984 with its 'Respublica Scotorum', and who, later, in 1990, the year that saw the publication of his enlarged *Collected Poems*, thought that politically:

> It is a very strange moment, when almost everyone believes some constitutional and/or other change is standing at the door, and necessarily so, yet a combination of nervous and nerveless hands seems unable to grasp the knob and open up.

Soon afterwards, in 1992, Morgan complained how 'we are up against a government that not only means to preserve the Union but is searching for ways to *strengthen* it, and one can only hope it overreaches itself in this, and thereby precipitates a broader discontent than manifests itself at the moment.' 'I don't believe "poetry makes nothing happen"', Morgan wrote in a letter of 1998, and six years later he was invited by Jack McConnell to become the inaugural Scottish Makar, going on to produce his poem 'For the Opening of the Scottish Parliament' on 9 October 2004. Morgan was too ill to read his poem (it was read by Liz Lochhead who would succeed him as Makar), but it stands as a signally successful piece of bardic oratory, a public poem of which Scotland remains proud:

> Open the doors! Light of the day, shine in; light of the mind, shine out!

Let me acknowledge again that the danger with the phrase 'bardic voice' is that it sounds old-fashioned, linked inextricably to Yeatsian 'last Romantics'. In Scotland, however, Morgan gave the lie to that, while still managing to draw on what he called the poetic 'resources of Scotland' as well as on an astonishingly wide range of poetic sustenance – from Gilgamesh to Ginsberg; and it was Morgan who in the penultimate dictated email of *The Midnight Letterbox* produced a tellingly astute statement on the public role of the poet as laureate; never a party hack (Morgan was not a joiner of political parties), he did attempt with grace a bardic voice, conscious of writing as a national poet at a time when:

> the people of Scotland… are, I think, quite certain of a movement in politics and society that is developing towards a very different way of looking at things – a Scottish as compared to an English way. The two nations (if we want to use that term) are still closely attached, but moving from that towards some kind of separation, although there may be argument about what degree of separation there should ultimately be.

Morgan's thoughts are too long to quote in full here, but are worth reading in *The Midnight Letterbox*. There he goes on to invoke the Hungarian national poet Petőfi and his 'National Song', before concluding that this work:

> was a reminder that a national poetry should not be involved in clinging to any particular political idea, or writing for money, and it is certainly not to be seen as a passing gift (whether granted by a queen or anyone else). Rather, poetry at this level should remind people that if they want to achieve something in the world, and to really be taken seriously, then they need to show the world what

they stand for. And surely those who are best equipped to articulate this are good writers, and this includes poets.

Though he certainly did not use the term, and though (as a gay man who had kept his sexuality secret for decades, and in other ways) he certainly understood the need for private voice, what Morgan is articulating here is the case for what I am calling 'bardic voice' in poetry. Bardic voice needs to be a crafted, sometimes unfashionably rhetorical tone of address; it should not be stuffy; it is present in Dunbar, in Burns, and in many other poets; and it remains a valid and urgent – though not the only valid and urgent – kind of voice to be heard today as it was in 2014 and has been for centuries before. To be a poet in Scotland now means to take the risk of bardic voice on occasion, not because we can be sure the work will last, but because of a deep desire to risk articulating something that matters. That's what led to some of us risking 'bardic voice' in 2014, and leads me still to stand by and to voice, both personally and inclusively, that risk.

Citations

'Cìocharan' by Marcas Mac an Tuairneir won first prize in the Scottish Association of Writers' 'Write Up North!' competition in 2015.

'Overheard on a bus in Aberdeen' by Mandy Macdonald previously appeared online in *I am not a silent poet*, iamnotasilentpoet.wordpress.com. The author extends her thanks to the editor Reuben Woolley.

'Picture of a Girl and Small Boy (Gaza, 2014)' by Marjorie Lotfi Gill previously appeared online as part of Rattle's Poets Respond series, www.rattle.com.

'leave behind' by Alec Finlay cites *Place-names of West Aberdeenshire* by James MacDonald, *The Dee From the Far Cairngorms* by Ian Murray, and *The Place Names of Upper Deeside* by Adam Watson.

'To Mohammed' by Henry Bell previously appeared as a Sacfree Press 'Poem-for-All'.

'Scottish Election Tongue Twister' by Henry Bell previously appeared in *The Glad Rag* published by the Glad Café.

'And So the People Spoke' by Anita John previously appeared on the website of Scottish PEN, scottishpen.org.

'Alice Coy Told Me How' by Henry Bell previously appeared on electronicintifada.net.

'For Refuge' by Pippa Little appeared in review in *MsLexia* Issue 70.

'Four Allegories of Independence' by Brian Johnstone was first published on NationalCollective.com and subsequently appeared in French translation by Stéphane Despatie in *Exit 77* (Montréal, Québec 2014); earlier versions of the individual poems were published in *The Herald* (Glasgow), *Poetry Scotland*, *Gutter* and *Lakeview Journal* (India).

Contributors

KATIE AILES is a poet and scholar based in Glasgow. In 2014–15 she completed an MRes in English at the University of Strathclyde on a US–UK Fulbright Award, focusing on poetry written for the 2014 Scottish independence referendum. In 2015 she co-organised the Poetic Politics conference at the National Library of Scotland. She is now pursuing her PhD at Strathclyde researching contemporary UK performance poetry. An active spoken word artist, Katie performs and organises with the Scottish collective Loud Poets. She is also a Clydebuilt poet (2015–16), co-editor of *Quotidian* literary magazine and co-pilot of the Scottish Poetry Library Ambassadors programme.

HENRY BELL is a writer and editor from Bristol, working on poetry and theatre. He lives on the Southside of Glasgow and edits *Gutter* magazine. He was a Clydebuilt poet, has had his work performed at Oran Mor and Summerhall and edited books including *Tip Tap Flat* and *A Bird is Not a Stone*. His writing has appeared in *Northwords Now, Raum, The Glasgow Review of Books, Bella Caledonia, Poems-for-all, Gutter* and *Type*. You can find out more at henryjimbell.com

HILARY BIRCH's family emigrated to New Zealand in 1958. A huge upheaval. Some of them returned to Scotland in 1970. More upheaval. Now in her twilight years, she lives in Edinburgh and enjoys various artistic and literary activities. Occasionally she writes poetry and finds it can release ideas and feelings that would otherwise remain mute.

JOHN BOLLAND writes novels, poetry and short fiction. He lives and works in the North East of Scotland. A graduate of Glasgow University's MLitt programme, he was runner-up in the V.S. Pritchett Short Story Prize and a prizewinner in the Fish International Short Story competition. His work has appeared in *Northwords Now*, *Lallans*, *The London Magazine*, *Pushing Out the Boat*, *Poetry Scotland*, *The Poets Republic* and a number of anthologies.

WILLIAM BONAR graduated MLitt in Creative Writing (Distinction) from Glasgow University in 2008 and he was tutored by Liz Lochhead as part of the 'North Star' cohort of the Clydebuilt apprenticeship scheme (2010–11). He was shortlisted in 2015 for a New Writers Award. His pamphlet, *Offering*, (available from www.redsquirrelpress.com), received the James Kirkup Memorial Award in 2014. His poems have been included in the Scottish Poetry Library's online anthology, *Best Scottish Poems*, for both 2012 and 2015. He is a founder member and committee member of St Mungo's Mirrorball, Glasgow's network of poets and lovers of poetry.

CHRIS BOYLAND is 44 years old. Although he has worked with different forms of writing over the years – including plays, short stories and television and film scripts – the two pieces included in this collection are his first published poems. He currently lives and works in central Scotland and enjoys performing at open mic poetry nights around Glasgow.

DAVID CAMERON was born in Glasgow in 1966. In 2014 he received the Hennessy Literary Award for Poetry – his collection *The Bright Tethers: Poems 1988–2016* is published by Rún Press. David is also the author of two books of fiction, *Rousseau Moon* (2000) and *The Ghost of*

Alice Fields (2014), both of which were chosen (by Robert Nye and Ron Butlin, respectively) among the Books of the Year in the Scottish press. David works as an instructional designer in Belfast. He is married to the Irish glass artist Louise Rice, and they have three young children.

GAVIN CAMERON was born in Dundee in 1983. He runs the writers' open mic night Hotchpotch in the city, and leads National Novel Writing Month for the Dundee & Angus region. Gavin's short stories have been published in England, Australia and the USA, while two of his poems will be included in the forthcoming *Seagate III* anthology. 'Crossing The Road' is his most personal piece to date.

JIM CARRUTH is the current poet Laureate of Glasgow. His most recent chapbook *Prodigal* was published in 2014 and won the Callum Macdonald Memorial award. His verse novella *Killochries* was published in 2015 and was shortlisted for the Saltire Award for Scottish poetry book of the year, the Fenton Aldeburgh Prize and the Seamus Heaney Centre Poetry Prize.

AC CLARKE is a poet living in Glasgow and a member of Scottish PEN. She is interested in outsiders and obscure historical figures. Her fourth collection, *In The Margin* (Cinnamon Press), came out last year and a pamphlet in Gaelic, Scots and English, *Owersettin*, in collaboration with Sheila Templeton and Maggie Rabatski, was published by Tapsalteerie this year. Her collection about the medieval visionary Margery Kempe has been accepted for publication by Oversteps Books.

ROBERT CRAWFORD's first full collection of poems in English, *A Scottish Assembly*, was published by Chatto & Windus in 1990 and his most recent collection is *Testament*

(Cape, 2014). His prose volumes include *Scotland's Books* (Penguin, 2007), *The Bard: Robert Burns, a Biography* (Cape, 2009) and *Young Eliot: From St Louis to 'The Waste Land'* (Cape, 2015). Recently he has edited *The Book of Iona* (Polygon, 2016) and collaborated with the photographer Norman McBeath on the Scots volume *Chinese Makars* (Easel Press, 2016). He is a professor in the School of English, University of St Andrews.

KATY EWING is a writer and artist based in south Scotland. She has had poetry, prose and illustration published in journals and anthologies including *New Writing Scotland*, *The Poets' Republic* and *Far Off Places* as well as being one of nine poets included in the forthcoming *House of Three* series of anthologies. She has also just completed an MLitt in Environment, Culture and Communication at the University of Glasgow.

ALEC FINLAY, born in 1966, is an internationally acclaimed artist and poet whose work crosses over a range of media and forms, from poetry, sculpture and collage, to audiovisual, new media and renewable technology. He has published over 30 books. Recent publications include *ebban an' flowan* (2015), *a better tale to tell* (2015), *I Hear Her Cry* (2015), *Global Oracle* (2014) and *Taigh: a wilding garden* (2014).

RONA FITZGERALD was born and educated in Dublin. She has been living in Glasgow for 21 years. Beginning with six poems in the Dublin-based *Stinging Fly* magazine in 2011, she has been published in UK and Scottish anthologies, in Scottish Book Trust publications and in both print and online magazines. Rona is a member of the Federation of Writers (Scotland), currently serving on the committee.

DAVID FORREST writes in both English and Scots, predominantly on the themes of love and worth with occasional forays into the politics of conflict, nationalism and trade. Much of his material can be found on his Facebook page 'David Forrest – Writer' or on his website, www.davidforrest.scot. He lives in Glasgow and frequently performs both there and further afield.

JANE FRANK is a poet and academic from Brisbane, Australia who lived in Scotland for a number of years in the 1990s. She is the author of *Milky Way of Words* (Ginninderra Press, 2016). Her poems have appeared in *Antipodes*, *Australian Poetry Journal*, *Westerly*, *Takahē*, *Writ*, *The Poets' Republic*, *Northwords Now* and elsewhere.

HARRY GILES is from Orkney and lives in Edinburgh. Harry's latest publication is the collection *Tonguit* from Freight Books, shortlisted for the 2016 Forward Prize for Best First Collection. Harry was the 2009 BBC Scotland slam champion, co-directs the live art platform ANATOMY and has toured participatory theatre across Europe and Leith. www.harrygiles.org

MARJORIE LOTFI GILL's work has won competitions, has been widely published in journals and anthologies including *The Rialto*, *Gutter*, *Magma* and *Rattle* and has been performed on BBC Radio 4. Marjorie was the first Poet in Residence at Jupiter Artland and the 2015 Writer in Residence for Spring Fling and the Wigtown Book Festival. Marjorie is also a co-founder of The Belonging Project, a series of workshops and readings reflecting on the flight, journey and assimilation of refugees. She presented this work and her own at both the 2016 Wigtown Book Festival and the 2016 Dundee Literary Festival.

IRENE HOSSACK teaches Creative Writing and English Language at The Open University. She studied at Monash University, Melbourne, writing her doctoral dissertation on the poetry and poetics of Geoffrey Hill. Her poetry has been published internationally over a number of years and she was tutored by Liz Lochhead as part of the 'North Star' cohort of St Mungo's Mirrorball Clydebuilt apprenticeship scheme (2010–11). Most recently her poem 'Cumbernauld' appears in the online project *Whaur Extremes Meet* https://scotiaextremis.wordpress.com/2016/04/11/week-12-cumbernauldpolphail/ and 'Fairy Liquid' in the *Double Bill* anthology published by Red Squirrel Press.

ANITA JOHN has an MSC in Creative Writing from Edinburgh University and is a Live Literature Scotland poet and short story writer. She has run creative writing courses for Edinburgh University, the RSPB Loch Leven and Abbotsford House. In 2013 she was selected as a Borders Showcase Poet by the Scottish Poetry Library and CABN. Her debut book *Child's Eye* is available from Amazon and more of her work can be found at anitajohn.co.uk

BRIAN JOHNSTONE is a poet, writer, and performer whose work has appeared throughout Scotland, elsewhere in the UK, in North America, and across Europe. He has published six collections, most recently *Dry Stone Work* (Arc, 2014). His poems have been translated into over a dozen languages. In 2015 his work was selected to appear on the Poetry Archive website. His memoir *Double Exposure* is due out from Saraband in 2017. A founder and former Director of StAnza: Scotland's International Poetry Festival, he has appeared at various poetry festivals, from Macedonia to Nicaragua, and at numerous venues across the UK. brianjohnstonepoet.co.uk

RUSSELL JONES is an Edinburgh-based writer and editor. He has published four collections of poetry, plus fiction, travel writing, and academic research. Russell is the deputy editor of *Shoreline of Infinity*, a science fiction magazine, *Where Rockets Burn Through: Contemporary Science Fiction Poems from the* UK and the forthcoming *Umbrellas of Edinburgh: Poetry and Prose Inspired by Scotland's Capital City*. Russell has a PhD in Creative Writing from The University of Edinburgh. He enjoys White Russians, Twiglets and karaoke.

DAVID KINLOCH was born, raised and educated in Glasgow, and currently serves as Professor of Poetry and Creative Writing at the University of Strathclyde. Kinloch is the author of five collections including *Finger of a Frenchman* (2011), *In My Father's House* (2005) and *Un Tour d'Ecosse* (2001), all published by Carcanet, and of many critical works in the fields of French, Translation and Scottish studies. He has been awarded the Robert Louis Stevenson Memorial Award (2004), a Scottish Writers' Bursary from the Scottish Arts Council (2006) and a Fellowship by the Arts and Humanities Research Council for his poetry (2013). He was a founder editor of the poetry magazine *Verse*, and has been instrumental in setting up the first Scottish Writers' Centre.

PIPPA LITTLE is Scots and lives in Northumberland where she is a Royal Literary Fund Fellow at Newcastle University. *Overwintering*, from OxfordPoets/Carcanet, came out in 2012 and was shortlisted for The Seamus Heaney Centre Prize. A new collection, *Twist*, is forthcoming from Arc. Her work has appeared in many print and online journals, on radio, and in film, and is anthologised widely. She teaches workshops in creative writing and takes an active role in the women's writing group she co-founded.

MARCAS MAC AN TUAIRNEIR writes in both Gaelic and English. His début collection was *Deò* (2013). His second, *Lus na Tùise*, and a novel, *Cuairteagan*, are forthcoming this year. In 2016 he was named New Gaelic Playwright of the year. Based in Inverness, he is a member of the Gaelic male-voice ensemble, Trosg. MarcasMac.co.uk and Trosg.com

Bidh MARCAS MAC AN TUAIRNEIR a' sgrìobhadh sa Ghàidhlig is sa Bheurla. B' e 'Deò' (2013) a' chiad chruinneachadh bàrdachd aige. Tha an dàrna fear 'Lus na Tùise', is a' chiad nobhail aige, 'Cuairteagan' rin tighinn am-bliadhna. Ann an 2016 choisinn e duais Dràmaire Ùr na Gàidhlig. Stèidhichte ann an Inbhir Nis, bidh e a' seinn am measg fireannaich eile na sgìre sa chòmhlan Ghàidhlig Trosg. MarcasMac.co.uk is Trosg.com

MANDY MACDONALD is an Australian writer living in Aberdeen and trying to make sense of the 21st and earlier centuries. Her poems have appeared in print in the anthologies *Outlook Variable* and *Extraordinary Forms* (Grey Hen Press, 2015), the *Maligned Species Project*, *Lunar Poetry*, *Poetry Scotland* and *Pushing Out the Boat*, and online in *The Fat Damsel*, *The Stare's Nest*, *Triadae*, *I am not a silent poet* and elsewhere. She writes in the strong hope that poetry can change the world, even just a little. The rest of the time, she sings.

MATTHEW MACDONALD is an award-winning multi-slam winning performance poet who has toured the UK and US and performed in the PBH Free Fringe since 2011. His debut pamphlet *Who Are Your People?* was released by Red Squirrel Press in July 2014 and his debut full length collection *petrichor* will be released in 2017. He performs regularly across Edinburgh and you can find more of his work at mattmacdonaldpoetry.wordpress.com (@MattMacPoet).

CALUM L MacLEÒID was born in Inverness and now lives in Montréal. In 2014 he won a New Writers Award from the Scottish Books Trust and the Gaelic Books Council. He also writes the Gaelic column for *The National*.

Rugadh CALUM L MacLEÒID ann an Inbhir Nis agus tha e a' fuireach ann am Montréal. Ann an 2014 choisinn e Duais nan Sgrìobhadairean ùra aig Comhairle nan Leabhraichean agus Urras Leabhraichean na h-Alba. Bidh e cuideachd a' sgrìobhadh colbh Gàidhlig anns a' phàipear naidheachd *The National*.

GREG MacTHÒMAIS is a short story writer/poet/librarian/ translator originally from Clydebank who has been living in Sleat in the Isle of Skye since 2000. He is a fluent Scottish Gaelic speaker, an enthusiastic Irish Gaelic learner and a fan of local devolution and Scottish independence. He won a Scottish Book Trust/Comhairle nan Leabhraichean 2015 New Writer award and his poems have appeared in *Northwords Now*, *New Writing Scotland* and *Causeway/Cabhsair*.

HUGH MCMILLAN is a poet from South West Scotland, a winner in The Scottish National Open Poetry Competition, The Smith/Doorstep Pamphlet Prize, the Callum MacDonald Prize and the Cardiff International Poetry Competition. He has also been shortlisted for the Michael Marks Prize and the Basil Bunting Award. His poetry has been published, anthologised and broadcast widely. His Selected Poems *Not Actually Being in Dumfries* were published by Luath Press in Edinburgh in 2015. His book *McMillan's Galloway* was published in 2016, also by Luath. He is currently working on a play about radical Galloway funded by Creative Scotland.

SARAH PATERSON is in her third and final year of a PHD in Scottish Literature at the University of Glasgow, thanks to the William Georgetti Scholarship. Originally from Dunedin, New Zealand, her poetry has appeared in New Zealand publications including *Critic*, *Takahē* and *Deep South* of which she was also the editor, and Scottish publications such as *Quaich* and *Quotidian*. She has worked for Otago Museum and Policy Scotland, and volunteered for UN Youth NZ and Maryhill Integration Network and in the Calais refugee camps. In 2015 she was a co-organiser of the Poetic Politics conference.

CALUM RODGER is a Glasgow-based poet and scholar. He performs widely throughout Scotland, including shows at the National Museum of Scotland and TEDxGlasgow, has two chapbooks (*Know Yr Stuff: Poems on Hedonism* and *Glasgow Flourishes*) published by Tapsalteerie Press, holds a PHD in Scottish Literature from the University of Glasgow and currently works part time as a prison librarian. Check out more of his work at www.calumrodger.co.uk.

STEWART SANDERSON was born in Glasgow in 1990. In 2015 he received an Eric Gregory Award. His first pamphlet is *Fios* (Tapsalteerie, 2015). He recently completed a PHD in Scottish Literature at the University of Glasgow, and is a 2016 Robert Louis Stevenson Fellow.

FINOLA SCOTT's poems and stories are widely published in anthologies and magazines including *The Ofi Press, Raum, The Lake, Poets Republic, The Eildon Tree* and *Poetry Scotland*. This year she is mentored on the Clydebuilt Scheme by Liz Lochhead. A performance poet, she is proud to be a slam-winning granny.

RODDY SHIPPIN is anti-war, anti-cuts and anti-histamine. He is based in Edinburgh, where he has spent the last few years living the arts graduate dream in a variety of call centres. His poems have appeared in such publications as *Gutter, Magma, Poetry Scotland* and *Northwords Now*. He helps to run the regular Edinburgh spoken word events Blind Poetics and Poets Against Humanity, as well as edit the poetry at *Valve Journal*.

NANCY SOMERVILLE, a Glaswegian who lives on the Isle of Mull, writes mainly poetry and short stories. Her poetry collection *Waiting for Zebras* was published by Red Squirrel Press (Scotland) in 2008. She has the first draft of a novel nagging at her to hurry up and get it finished.

ARUN SOOD is a writer and academic. He was born and raised in Scotland to a Gaelic-speaking, West-Highland mother and Punjabi-Indian father. He travels often, and at any opportunity, but holds a strong spiritual (and ancestral) tie to the North-West Highlands and Islands.

ROSS WILSON comes from Kelty, a former mining village in West Fife, and lives in Condorrat, North Lanarkshire. His poems and short stories have been widely published, his lyrics set to music and recorded by folk trio The Sairbanes, and he contributed to the script of *The Happy Lands* (2013), an acclaimed award-winning feature film in which he was credited as an actor. His first pamphlet collection, *The Heavy Bag*, was published by Calder Wood Press in 2011 and his first full collection will be published by Smokestack Books in 2018. He works as an Auxiliary Nurse in Glasgow.

VALERIE WILSON was born and brought up in the Southside of Edinburgh, though she now lives in East Lothian. She worked for Edinburgh District, Lothian Region and City of Edinburgh Council until she was medically retired after her eldest son's murder. After her book *Facets in Poetry* was published in 1998, the publisher went bust and the books are no longer in production. Valerie has poems in three non-paying anthologies: *The Lyre's Song, Touching Tributes* and *Laughter In The Midst*. The brash angst poetry reflects the raw emotion of her life whilst in other poems her sense of humour is evinced.

Some other books published by **LUATH** PRESS

Scotia Nova

Poems for the early days of a better nation
Edited by Alistair Findlay and Tessa Ransford
ISBN: 978-1-910021-10-1 PBK £8.99

great piers stride the firth like chessmen, whiles the scrivvers scrive

– Read these poems and be inspired.

Scotland's Independence Referendum on 18 September 2014 resounded with claims from all sides that a better Scotland is not only possible but necessary, whether remaining with the Union or leaving it. Scotland's artists and writers have long cultivated a distinct and independent cultural tradition undimmed – indeed frequently provoked – by political union. The project remains unfinished as the country heads towards totally unprecedented territory. The only sure thing seems to be that the political status quo is not an option, the only question being the extent of the changes ahead.

This is a confident, upbeat collection, drawing on shared history and language... invoking the ghosts of Hugh MacDiarmid, Margo MacDonald, Naomi Mitchison, Burns and Lenin.
ANDY CROFT, Morning Star

The majority of the poems are successful. At its strongest moments it is a testament to the richness of Scottish poetry, and serves as a detailed snapshot of the nation.
MICHAEL GRIEVE, The Saint

100 Favourite Scottish Poems

Edited by Stewart Conn
ISBN: 1 905222 61 0 PBK £7.99

Poems to make you laugh. Poems to make you cry. Poems to make you think. Poems to savour. Poems to read out loud. To read again, and again. Scottish poems. Old favourites. New favourites. 100 of the best.

Scotland has a long history of producing outstanding poetry. From the humblest but-and-ben to the grandest castle, the nation has a great tradition of celebration and commemoration through poetry. *100 Favourite Scottish Poems* – incorporating the top 20 best-loved poems as selected by a BBC Radio Scotland listener poll – ranges from ballads to Burns, from 'Proud Maisie' to 'The Queen of Sheba', and from 'Cuddle Doon' to 'The Jeelie Piece Song'.

Edited by Stewart Conn, poet and inaugural recipient of the Institute of Contemporary Scotland's Iain Crichton Smith Award for services to literature (2006).

Details of these and other books published by Luath Press
can be found at: **www.luath.co.uk**

Luath Press Limited
committed to publishing well written books worth reading

LUATH PRESS takes its name from Robert Burns, whose little collie Luath (*Gael.*, swift or nimble) tripped up Jean Armour at a wedding and gave him the chance to speak to the woman who was to be his wife and the abiding love of his life.

Burns called one of 'The Twa Dogs' Luath after Cuchullin's hunting dog in Ossian's *Fingal*. Luath Press was established in 1981 in the heart of Burns country, and now resides a few steps up the road from Burns' first lodgings on Edinburgh's Royal Mile.

Luath offers you distinctive writing with a hint of unexpected pleasures.

Most bookshops in the UK, the US, Canada, Australia, New Zealand and parts of Europe either carry our books in stock or can order them for you. To order direct from us, please send a £sterling cheque, postal order, international money order or your credit card details (number, address of cardholder and expiry date) to us at the address below. Please add post and packing as follows: UK – £1.00 per delivery address; overseas surface mail – £2.50 per delivery address; overseas airmail – £3.50 for the first book to each delivery address, plus £1.00 for each additional book by airmail to the same address. If your order is a gift, we will happily enclose your card or message at no extra charge.

Luath Press Limited
543/2 Castlehill
The Royal Mile
Edinburgh EH1 2ND
Scotland

Telephone: 0131 225 4326 (24 hours)
email: sales@luath.co.uk
Website: www.luath.co.uk